Humour and Horror

twelve short plays by
Ken Blakeson
J. C. W. Brook
David Campton
William Humble
Jill Hyem
Maurice Patterson
Sam Smith
Peter Terson
Peter Whalley
Ted Willis
J. C. Wilsher
R. D. Wingfield

selected and edited by
Caroline Bennitt

photographs by
Catherine Shakespeare Lane

Longman

LONGMAN GROUP LIMITED
Longman House
Burnt Mill, Harlow, Essex, CM20 2JE, England and Associated
Companies throughout the World.
Plays © the respective playwrights
This edition © Longman Group Limited 1985

*All rights reserved. No part of this publication may be
reproduced, stored in a retrieval system, or transmitted in any
form or by any means, electronic, mechanical, photocopying,
recording or otherwise, without the prior written permission of
the Publisher.*

First published 1985

ISBN 0 582 22391 1

Set in 10/11 pt Baskerville, Linotron 202

Printed in Hong Kong by
Commonwealth Printing Press Ltd

En Attendant François
No performance or reading of *En Attendant François* by David
Campton may be given unless a licence has been obtained in
advance from the author's agents ACTAC Ltd, 16 Cadogan Lane,
London SW1 and no copy of the play or any part therefore may
be reproduced for any purpose whatsoever by any printing or
photographic or other method without written permission
obtained in advance from the publishers. Non-observance of the
above stipulations constitutes a breach of copyright.

Contents

Introduction

Short radio plays have several advantages for the classroom: they can be 'performed' with a minimum of preparation; everyone can be involved in studying a part which is important but not lengthy; and presentation and discussion can take place within a single teaching period.

These plays have been selected from a Radio 4 series called *Just Before Midnight*, and most have a hint of the macabre or supernatural, frequently with an element of humour. Some are merely entertaining, while others are more disturbing and thought-provoking; but all have good parts, dramatic situations, and interesting points for discussion.

Although written primarily to be heard but not seen, many would translate easily onto a simple stage with a few props and costumes – notably *Maniacs, En Attendant François, Tick Tock, And No Birds Sing*, and *The Bognor Regis Vampire*. The more complicated ones like *Nightmare* and *Susie Graham's Dance Trophy* can provide a challenging exercise for those interested in the techniques of sound recording.

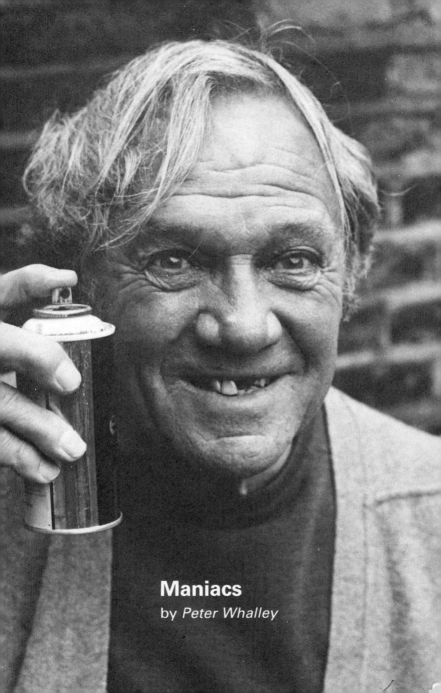

Maniacs

by *Peter Whalley*

The Cast

George *the boilerman, early sixties, aggressive, self-confident*
Fred *the groundsman, late forties, slow, gentle*
Mr Fish *the headmaster, young, well-educated, polite*

Behind the gruesome scenes at a ghastly comprehensive, Fred and George bemoan the weakness of the teachers and the vandalism, hooliganism and promiscuity of the pupils. Mr Fish seems to think all is well, but Fred and George have their own ideas for dealing with the worst offenders.

Maniacs

A school boiler-house

The boiler is heard faintly throughout.

GEORGE Can I offer you some tea this morning, Fred? Or have you got your flask?

FRED Oh, I've got me flask.

GEORGE I thought you would have.

FRED It's useful if I'm over by t'cricket square. Saves trekking back here.

GEORGE Hang on a minute.

He moves away. We hear him fill a kettle and switch it on.

(*distant*) And why do we need a cricket square in November? Or is that a state secret?

FRED You need one in November so that you can have one July following.

GEORGE (*returning*) Then why have one at all, eh? I mean the time that you, as groundsman, have to put into that. Why have one at all?

FRED I suppose it's to play cricket on.

GEORGE Well, there's no denying that. Would you like an eccles cake?

FRED No thanks, George. I've got me pipe.

GEORGE No, what I mean is, what does a school that caters exclusively for the ungrateful, the unwashed and the downright bloody unspeakable want with a cricket square? Now a barracks square — I could understand that.

FRED They won't have any sort of square left by the next year if I don't get on top of that moss.

GEORGE They don't even wear proper flannels. What I've seen of 'em. Denims they wear. Denims. Next year I daresay it'll be swimming trunks.

FRED It were swimming trunks last year.

GEORGE My God.

FRED And pads. They're not allowed to play without pads.

GEORGE Not allowed! They're allowed to do owt they want. (*Pause*) Used to be a game for gentlemen did cricket. Mind you so did a lot of things. And what happened, eh?

FRED To cricket?

GEORGE To everything. At what point did the scum rise to cover the surface?

FRED Oh aye.

GEORGE And why did we allow it, eh? Why did we allow 'em to take over everything? Streets, football grounds, shopping precincts.

FRED Cricket squares.

GEORGE The worst thing this country ever did was to end national service[1].

FRED There were a gang of 'em out there again this morning. I don't know what lesson they were supposed to be doing.

GEORGE Rural studies.

FRED I don't know.

GEORGE It'd be rural studies. He sends 'em out. Look into the distance, he says, and see what you can see. And that's the lesson.

FRED Well, they just look to be hanging about to me. Till they saw that I were sweeping leaves up off tennis courts.

GEORGE Hang on. Me kettle's boiling.

He moves away.

FRED Then they came and started kicking all t'leaves about. The piles I'd made. Just kicking 'em about. Great lads of fifteen or sixteen.

George returns with the kettle and makes his tea.

GEORGE What, the leaves that you'd collected?

FRED They kept shouting, "Who loves you[2], Fred! Who loves you, Fred!"

GEORGE Mental.

---

1 two years' compulsory military training for boys   2 catchphrase from the popular American TV detective series *Kojak*

FRED   Great, gangling yobs. Fifteen or sixteen. Who loves you, Fred! You wouldn't credit it.

GEORGE   Mental they are. Want locking up, most of 'em.

FRED   When I'd go to sweep em up again, they'd go, "Leave the leaves, Fred! Leave the leaves!"

GEORGE   Barbarians. The new barbarians of the Welfare State. Pouring out of comprehensive schools everywhere.

FRED   Aye. Though I suppose . . .

GEORGE   What?

FRED   Well, I sometimes think they can't be *all* that bad. Not every last one.

GEORGE   You'd think not, wouldn't you, but . . . (*he sighs*)

FRED   Some of the girls aren't unpleasant.

GEORGE   And some of 'em are worse than the flaming lads. Some of 'em. Dirty little devils some of 'em.

FRED   Oh aye.

GEORGE   You ought to listen to the wife after she's cleaned the girls' toilets of a night.

FRED   Aye, it can't be a picnic cleaning them.

GEORGE   It's an indictment[1] of what modern education's all about, Fred. It is. The combination of literacy and sex education has reeked havoc over them walls. And what's astonishing is the way that their spelling picks up when they come to t'dirty words. I don't know how to account for that, do you?

FRED   No.

GEORGE   No. You're sure you won't have this eccles cake? She always puts me two in.

FRED   No, ta, George. I'll stick to me pipe.

GEORGE   You know we can sometimes spend two hours of a night talking about us experiences. Her with her cleaning and me with my caretaking. Sometimes I think they should change that board outside so that it says Sodom and Gomorrah[2] High School.

FRED   The sights I see over by the long jump pit.

GEORGE   I'll bet.

FRED   The sights I've seen there.

GEORGE   They should be gelded[3]. Most of 'em. Gelded when they come into t' first year. At that age they wouldn't

---

1 condemnation   **2** two evil cities destroyed by God: *Genesis* 19   **3** castrated like horses know what they were missing.

FRED Well, I've stopped bothering about it. I mean, they don't bother. So why should I?

GEORGE Oh, they don't. If I ever stop a couple of 'em at it behind this boiler-house, I get a right mouthful in return.

FRED If I'm out with tractor I just carry straight on till they move.

GEORGE How did we ever get to this stage, eh?

He lights a cigarette.

FRED I reckon I've stopped a few babies that way.

GEORGE A tide of filth is what we face, Fred. A tide of filth and ignorance. Ever since Mr Fletcher went.

FRED Fletcher.

GEORGE The finest headmaster this school has ever had.

FRED Before my time he was.

GEORGE Wonderful man. The kids walked in fear of him. Terrified they were. And the staff for that matter.

FRED Aye?

GEORGE I'll tell you what. He'd have put paid to one or two of these young thugs that we have swaggering about here.

(Pause)

FRED Knackenhead.

George gives a small cry and we hear the crash of his cup to the floor.

GEORGE Oh, look at that now!

FRED Sorry, George.

GEORGE Damn. And I've had that cup for, what, must be five year.

FRED Sorry, George.

GEORGE Nay. You took me by surprise, that's all. I wasn't prepared for it. For the name. Knackenhead.

FRED It just put me in mind of him when you said . . .

GEORGE Oh yes, yes.

FRED Would you like a drop from me flask? There's a spare beaker on it.

GEORGE Aye. Go on then.

And we hear Fred pour it.

(*joking*) Steady me nerves. I mean the thought of him's worse than any horror film.

FRED (*giving him the tea*) There.

GEORGE Ta.

FRED He should have had an X-certificate[1] hung round his neck.

GEORGE Aye. The ultimate in horror. Frankenstein, Dracula and King Kong meet Knackenhead!

They both have a quiet laugh.

(*turning serious*) Still, it's no joke though, it it? A great lout like that loose around t'corridors. And with most of teachers scared of him.

FRED Oh aye.

GEORGE That's why they send him out so often. Out of classes. Mind you, he looked a sight in 'em.

FRED I'll bet he did.

GEORGE I once went into, oh, Mrs Quincey's class it were. You know, little twitchy woman, teaches art.

FRED Drives a Mini.

GEORGE Yes.

FRED Keeps a Yorkshire terrier.

GEORGE That's her. Well, I went into her class to fetch a step-ladder. She'd borrowed it for a still life. And it were still an' all. Two weeks later it were still there. So I went to retrieve it. Well, minute I opened door they all started yelling out.

FRED Oh aye.

GEORGE You know the sort of thing.

FRED I do.

GEORGE All right, George! Going up in the world, George! All that kind of crap. Anyway, in't middle, there sat Knackenhead leering at me and mouthing obscenities.

FRED I can imagine.

GEORGE But I had to smile to meself, you know. Seeing him there, this great six foot two article, dressed like a circus parade . . .

FRED A punk.

GEORGE Aye. Though I would imagine even other punks found him offensive. Anyway, there he was, all squeezed in

1 Film for adults only

behind this little desk. And holding a pen – My God, I thought, I've seen everything now – holding a pen in his great fist. I'm not kidding, it were like seeing, you know, an elephant at a circus doing tricks. Unnatural.

FRED He should have been down a coal-mine.

GEORGE He should have been down a coal-mine from the age of five. But no, he has to go to school.

FRED Aye.

GEORGE Only teachers won't have him in their classes. So they send him out.

FRED Aye.

GEORGE And where does he end up? Where does Knackenhead go when he's sent out of classes because his teachers are all scared rigid of him?

FRED Down here.

GEORGE Right. Down here in this boiler-room. *My* boiler-room if you please.

FRED They always do, don't they?

GEORGE Like a magnet this place is to 'em. All the thugs and the louts and the yobbos. I could run a borstal down here with the visitors I get.

FRED You could.

GEORGE Dirty, filthy yobbos hanging about, smoking their fags and telling their dirty, crude stories to one another.

FRED Well, it's somewhere warm, isn't it? In winter. When it's summer they come digging up my cricket square.

GEORGE They come barging their way in. Let's have a warm, George. Got any dirty books for us, George? Getting it regular, are you, George?

FRED Aye, and it's funny how . . .

GEORGE Effing and blinding as though I weren't here! As though I were deaf!

FRED Aye.

GEORGE Maniacs.

FRED And it's funny how you get one that stands out every year, isn't it?

GEORGE Like Knackenhead.

FRED This year yes. The pick of this year's crop, Knackenhead.

GEORGE Spitting on my floor. Spitting like old feller chewing tobacco.

FRED Aye.

8

GEORGE   Spit, spit, spit! It's a wonder they're not dehydrated, some of 'em.

FRED   There's always one though. Do you remember Slack?

GEORGE   Slack! Do I remember Slack!

FRED   Pick of last year's crop were Slack.

GEORGE   Slack with his aerosol cans.

FRED   He made a grand mess of my cricket pavilion.

GEORGE   He made a grand mess of anything he got twenty yards of did that ugly little runt. D'you see that up there?

FRED   What?

GEORGE   On that wall. Still there. I couldn't get it off.

FRED   Oh aye.

GEORGE   That were Slack. I once said to him, "Do you spray your walls at home? Do you go round doing that at home?"

FRED   What did he say?

GEORGE   I'll not repeat what he said, Fred. I won't. Though the gist of it was that he would aerosol whatever took his fancy and that my questions were not welcome. That was the gist of it.

(*Pause*)

FRED   Well, I've a hockey pitch to mark out before dinner time.

GEORGE   Course you know who I blame. You know why we have to put up with these maniacs spitting and smoking and foulmouthing in my boiler-house?

FRED   Teachers.

GEORGE   Well, don't you think so?

FRED   Oh aye.

GEORGE   They can't cope, can they? I mean, can you see little twitchy Mrs Quincey handling Knackenhead?

RED   Or Slack.

GEORGE   Or Slack. She wouldn't have a cat-in-hell's chance. Slack'd cover her in rude words from head to foot with his aerosol while Knackenhead 'd stand there chewing on her Yorkshire terrier,

A door opens and closes as Mr Fish enters.

(*whispering*) Eh up. Here's the man at the top.

MR FISH   (*approaching*) Morning George. Fred.

GEORGE   Mr Fish.

FRED   Morning.

MR FISH   Don't let me disturb you if you're having your break. Only when you've a minute, George, I wonder if you can do something about the chairs in the hall. I think I've mentioned it to you before . . .

GEORGE   I've been meaning to get round to it.

MR FISH   Oh yes. Yes. I'm not suggesting . . .

GEORGE   It's on me list. Only do you know, Mr Fish, that I spent two hours last night clearing mud from the ceilings of the teaching block.

MR FISH   Really, yes.

GEORGE   From the ceilings! I mean I know we've got some very clever individuals in this school but I didn't know any of 'em could walk on the ceilings.

MR FISH   No. (*Intrigued*) What, er, what exactly is it that they're doing?

GEORGE   Flicking.

MR FISH   Flicking?

GEORGE   Flicking mud balls.

MR FISH   Ah, I see.

GEORGE   Which then stick and dry out. Two hours it took me going round with a step-ladder and a paint-scraper.

MR FISH   Yes. Yes, I can see that it must be a problem. And I'm not sure just what the answer is.

GEORGE   Dirty little devils.

FRED   And that mud'll be taken from off my cricket square.

MR FISH   Well, er, leave that one with me, George. I'll alert the staff to what's going on.

GEORGE   I would be grateful.

MR FISH   Hmm. Anyway, these chairs. As I say, one or two are a bit worse for wear and I wondered if you could . . . have a go at them.

GEORGE   Whoever designed them chairs wants his head examining.

MR FISH   Really? Are they not, er, all they might be?

GEORGE   There are two screws just underneath your . . . just underneath the seat. And if you take them out the whole thing falls to bits.

MR FISH   Oh yes. Yes, I'm aware of that.

GEORGE   Well, all they need is a nail-file or a penknife and . . .

MR FISH   Oh yes, yes. But I've spelled it out. In assembly to the whole school. I explained about the screws and what happens if they are removed.

GEORGE   Oh well, at least they'll know how to do it properly then, won't they?

(*Pause*)

MR FISH   Hmm. Well, if you could get some screws from the craft block and have a go. Otherwise I fear that assembly will continue to be punctuated by the sound of falling bodies. And how are you, Fred? Everything all right, is it?

FRED   Not too bad, thank you.

MR FISH   Did we get those rugby posts back, could you just remind me? I think we got to the bottom of that one, didn't we?

FRED   Yes, in a manner of speaking.

MR FISH   Good, good. I wouldn't want you to feel that you didn't have our full support in these matters.

FRED   Chopped up.

MR FISH   What?

FRED   Posts. They came back chopped up. I've got 'em piled up now behind the pavilion. Longest piece isn't above two foot.

MR FISH   Ah. And there's no chance of sticking ...? No, I suppose not. Well, we'll have to see if the PTA[1] can help us out.

GEORGE   I know it's not my place to say it, Mr Fish, but the louts that we have here don't deserve the facilities they're given.

MR FISH   Oh ...

GEORGE   Maniacs most of 'em. Destroy anything they can get their hands on. I'm not saying the teaching staff's to blame, don't get me wrong ...

MR FISH   Oh, I think you're being a bit hard on the children there, George. I think I'd have to quarrel with you on that one.

GEORGE   With all due respect, Headmaster, you don't see 'em like we do.

---

1 Parent Teacher Association, which organises fund-raising activities to supply extra school equipment.

MR FISH   Well, I do spend a lot of time walking around this school and I must say I get immense satisfaction from seeing all the good work that goes on. I can walk down a corridor and there's a French class here, a History class there, they're dissecting something in Biology, baking something over here, studying the Russian Revolution over there . . .

GEORGE   And flicking mud balls at the ceiling.

Mr Fish manages an unconvincing laugh.

MR FISH   Oh, we do have . . . we do have our recalcitrants[1]. One or two wayward souls who haven't yet seen the light.

GEORGE   Well, that's as may be, but some of the language and behaviour that we have to put up with . . . eh, Fred?

FRED   Has to be seen to be believed.

GEORGE   And perhaps you don't see it, Mr Fish.

MR FISH   Well, I, er, I do try and spread myself as far as possible . . .

GEORGE   Real rogues' gallery we have sometimes in here. Isn't that right, Fred?

FRED   Aye.

MR FISH   Well, I can't deny that some of our lost souls may fetch up on your shores. I suppose this is something of a sanctuary for some of them.

GEORGE   You can say that again.

MR FISH   But you mustn't let that prejudice you against our worthy citizens, George. And they are in the majority. I can assure you of that.

GEORGE   Well, I'll take your word for that. But it's the rotten apples – isn't it – it's the rotten apples that turn all the rest. Unless you get 'em out in time.

MR FISH   Except that we are not, after all, we are not dealing with apples, are we? Oh, I'll tell you something that might cheer you up a bit. Relevant to what we've been talking about. You know . . . Knackenhead?

GEORGE   Oh yes.

FRED   Unfortunately.

MR FISH   Yes, I think he might rate as one of your rotten apples, mightn't he?

---

1 stubbornly disobedient ones

GEORGE To the bloody core that one.

MR FISH Well, I think with a bit of luck you might not be bothered with him for a while.

GEORGE Oh?

MR FISH Seems he's run away from home. Mother rang this morning. She hasn't seen him since the day before yesterday.

GEORGE Well, that's the best news I've heard for a long while.

MR FISH Yes, I think there'll be a few fingers crossed that he doesn't hurry back to the maternal bosom. Anyway, I'll leave you to it. (*Then coyly as he departs*) You won't forget the chairs, will you?

We hear the door close as he exits.
A moment's silence, then George laughs softly.

GEORGE Well, that's one rotten apple that won't spoil the barrel.

FRED Aye.

GEORGE You've cleaned that spade up, haven't you?

FRED Yes, yes. Clean as a new pin.

George laughs again.

GEORGE You know I didn't tell you, did I? Mrs Quincey stopped me yesterday. Said, "Oh, thank you, George, I don't know what you did to the boiler but it's the first day I've been properly warm since we've been back this term." And you know what she's usually like, all twitchy and starved to death.

FRED Aye.

GEORGE First day I've been properly warm, she said. I nearly told her, "Well, you've got Knackenhead to thank for that, love. He's providing the fuel!"

Fred laughs.

FRED First useful thing he's done.

GEORGE And the last.

(*Pause*)

FRED Well, I'll get on with that hockey pitch.

GEORGE And I'd better look at his damn silly chairs. Before he bursts into tears over 'em.

FRED I'll tell you what though, George.

GEORGE What's that, Fred?

FRED There's never been one as good as Slack, eh?

GEORGE What, you mean for giving off heat like?

FRED Well, it weren't that so much as throwing all his aerosol cans in after him. Hearing 'em explode inside boiler.

George laughs.

Little squirt.

GEORGE And what was that one before him? Pilkington?

FRED Summat like that. You forget their names after a time. They're that much alike.

GEORGE Aye. All wanting to be near t'boiler. Wanting a warm.

They both laugh.[1]
The door opens.

MR FISH (*from the door*) Er, sorry . . .

GEORGE Eh up.

MR FISH Sorry to pop back like this, chaps, but I thought I should warn you. Knackenhead has returned to us.

GEORGE (*quietly*) Oh God!

MR FISH Yes, I'm afraid so.

FRED Couldn't we have a whip-round? Send him off somewhere again?

MR FISH Walked up to me as bold as brass. All right boss, he said, I just couldn't keep away from your nice little prison.

He gives an uncertain laugh.

Quite a sense of humour really.

FRED For a gorilla.

GEORGE I thought he'd left home?

MR FISH Perhaps he got homesick . . .?

George and Fred give way to gloomy laughter.

(*not pleased*) Well, I'll . . . I'll leave you to get on with your work.

He exits. Their laughter dies.

GEORGE Knackenhead!

1 the play's original ending

FRED   Returned.

       (*Pause*)

GEORGE   If only we could, eh?

FRED   Aye.

GEORGE   Fight back. Take up arms against Knackenhead and his tribe!

FRED   We'd lose up pensions.

GEORGE   Oh, it wouldn't be understood. Wouldn't be well-received in the local press.

FRED   They can't stop us dreaming though.

GEORGE   No.

FRED   No.

GEORGE   Sweet dreams, eh? Sweet bloody dreams!

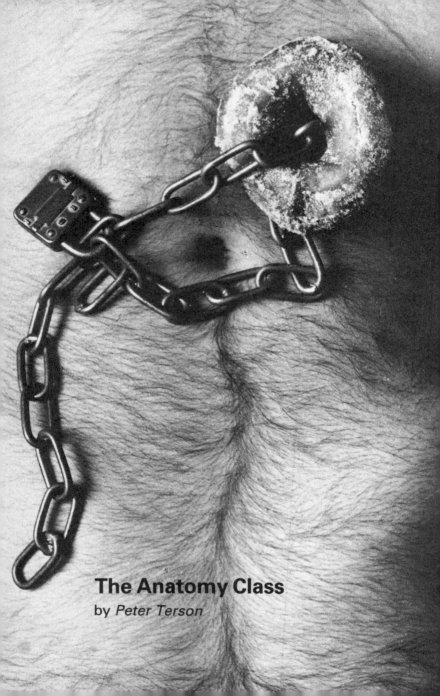

The Anatomy Class

by *Peter Terson*

The Cast

Jarvis *sarcastic, self-confident and cynical*
Jane *earnest admirer of the lecturer*
Sally *concerned with her boyfriend and her parents*
Martin *aspiring revue director and performer*
Frances *studious, interested and dedicated*
Terry *disorganised and insecure*
Lecturer *practised, suave and witty*

The thoughts of six medical students during a dissection of the stomach reveal what else is on their minds besides studying.

Some device, such as a microphone or a different voice pitch, is needed to distinguish "thoughts" from "aloud".

The Anatomy Class

A lecture room

Sound of students entering.

JARVIS   Morning cerebrals[1]. Anatomy, isn't it? (*Thoughts*) All we have to do for this one is put the feet up, head back and sweet dreams. (*Aloud*) Move along the bus.

JANE   Morning, Team . . . (*Thoughts*) Now – where shall I sit? Come off it Jane, you know exactly where you'll sit. Wherever you'll make the biggest impression.

SALLY   Room next to you Jane?

JANE   Bit tight, but welcome.

SALLY   (*sitting*) How did you get on last night?

JANE   At what?

SALLY   Not telling?

JANE   Don't even remember. (*Thoughts*) Nothing to remember.

SALLY   Can't have been very momentous.

JANE   So few of them are my dear, so few of them are.

SALLY   (*thoughts*) Why do I always sit beside her? I'm not *really* interested in her tawdry goings on.

JANE   Your mother been in touch recently?

SALLY   Oh shut up!

MARTIN   Morning all. No answer was the unanimous reply. (*Sits*) How boring is this one going to be Jarvis? I've just woken up, it won't need much to send me back.

JARVIS   Bouncy lad like *you* can keep awake. Martin.

MARTIN   Ah – but will I be able to concentrate?

JARVIS   The secret of attending lectures is the ability to concentrate on something else at the same time, so you don't become narrow minded.

MARTIN   Like on what?

JARVIS   Like on those two pieces of crumpet sitting down

---

1 brainy people

there together. Two well-stacked mounds of luscious flesh. Pity Sally's wasted with that feller from the engineering school.

MARTIN There ought to be a law that none of the crumpet should be allowed to change faculty until we've all had her... Morning Frances...

FRANCES (*approaching*) Morning. Is there a place there?

JARVIS If you wish to sit among the rowdies...

FRANCES Well if you insist on pretending to be a rowdy so be it...

MARTIN Touché my dear, touché ... come on Terry take your bicycle clips off ... you're not on the track now.

TERRY (*approaching*) Got caught in the jam[1]. (*Thoughts*) Late again. They're all in.

MARTIN I've warned you about taking condiments[2] at breakfast.

JARVIS Do we have to have corn[3] quite so early in the morning? Come on Terry, cheer us up...

TERRY Roll along the aisle[4] there please ... (*Thoughts*) Anatomy, God I wish I'd done some background reading for this one.

MARTIN Come on cheer leader...

FRANCES Could we do without the chat please? The professor's arrived.

JARVIS Shall we stand to attention, or beat a Double Hernia...

FRANCES We know you're clever, Jarvis, why tarnish it with third rate wit?

JARVIS You're such a wonderful girl Frances ... a perfect model[5] ... if only they'd made a humorous version[6].

LECTURER Good morning everyone ... could I have a little quiet now please.

TERRY (*thoughts*) Well, here goes ... it should be simple but I've got a feeling it'll be another hurdle I might just manage to tipple over.

LECTURER Today, I'm going to demonstrate a dissection of the abdomen. With special reference to the intestinal tract.

---

1 traffic queue   2 flavourings – such as jam   3 cereal; boring jokes
4 "move along the bus" + "roll in the aisle" = make room for me and collapse laughing
5 beauty; type of car   6 one of you; alternative design of car

JARVIS   That's it Prof, make it gutsy.

TERRY   Where's my pencil. (*Thoughts*) Nerves straining at the leash, he's always fast off the blocks this feller.

JARVIS   For crying out loud Terry, stop mumbling ... you're like a well-trained dolphin.

TERRY   I wish this place would warm up ... it's chilly after that ride in.

MARTIN   Another rotten Anatomy lecture, if we get one more this week, I'll turn into a cadaver. (*Thoughts*) This place needs livening up ... what we need is to put on another play ...

LECTURER   If I can just point out that the margin of the rib cage is the upper border of the abdomen and the skin creases in the groin and pubis act as the lower border I'm going to make my incision in the mid lines ... So, to begin ...

MARTIN   (*thoughts*) By all means let us begin. "To begin at the beginning." We could do *Under Milk Wood*. No, we get enough of the Welsh after rugby on Saturdays.

JARVIS   (*thoughts*) Look at them all; earnest beavers, scorching through their jotters. Have they no minds of their own any of them?

TERRY   (*thoughts*) If I took to Public Transport I suppose I wouldn't *sweat* like this ...

FRANCES   (*thoughts*) Let's see, we're doing head and neck at the end of this term ... I'll make a note of that ...

SALLY   (*thoughts*) Fancy Mum phoning when I was with Rodney, I wish she'd leave me alone ...

JANE   (*thoughts*) He looks so dignified down there ... and so alone ... I wonder if he's aware of us really? Or are we just a whelpish[1] mass beneath his notice?

LECTURER   The first thing you will see once I'm inside the abdominal cavity is a large fatty apron called the omentum; this is known as the abdominal policeman because whenever there is trouble in the abdomen the omentum wraps itself around the offending organ.

FRANCES   (*thoughts*) That should raise a smirk from the chorus. (*reaction*) Yes, there it goes.

TERRY   (*thoughts*) I'm getting lost already, he must be

1 puppy-like

somewhere between my teeth and my toes.

SALLY (*thoughts*) Talking about offending organs I could nip across to the Engineering School to see Rodney after this, if he doesn't go on too long ... I'll go via the letter rack in case Mum has sent another weepy ...

TERRY (*thoughts*) I wish he wouldn't give me that questioning look ... he always seems about to pounce. "You there, tell me the attachments of the greater Omentum ..." That would put me on the chopping block.

JARVIS (*thoughts*) Look at Jane, what a pair ... When she came to the dance she was so low cut she defied gravity ...

JANE (*thoughts*) How lonely he looks down there. Vulnerable ... among all these jokers. I wonder if he *is* vulnerable?

JARVIS (*thoughts*) It's Frances we have to beware of though. That sincerity would be lethal in the nude ...

FRANCES (*thoughts*) How I hate the air of studied indifference they all adopt. There's not one of them who isn't eaten up by fear of failing ... except Jarvis of course ... and perhaps Martin.

MARTIN (*thoughts*) I'd like to put on another show. We could put on an Agatha Christie who-dunnit. Get the Prof to supply the blood ... No, too corny. Sorry Agatha, move over baby, on to the next slab.

LECTURER (*aloud*) The omentum hangs from the lower border of the stomach which you will notice at the top. If I pull the stomach down you will see that the oesophagus comes through the diaphragm and enters the stomach.

JARVIS (*thoughts*) Quite a flashy bit of plumbing there Prof ... spends a load of time on a simple incision then streaks over a load of useful detail.

TERRY (*thoughts*) I wish he'd give us a few diagrams and lecture notes ... I can't hold this lot in my mind ... oh help – did I lock my bike?

SALLY (*thoughts*) Mum and Dad seemed glad enough when I left home ... to get a bit of middle-aged peace I suppose ... and twilight sex life ... but why these phone calls? What went wrong?

FRANCES (*thoughts*) This would be a super subject if only we could approach it differently ... *Exams* have to play the lead all the time ...

JANE (*thoughts*) Why is Frances so earnest? They all laugh about her, but with her potential she could leave them standing ... if only she would put personality before persuasion ...

LECTURER To the left, under the ribs, is the spleen[1], often vented[2] wastefully in Western Civilisation but more vulnerable in the Far East ...

MARTIN (*thoughts*) This bloke's got potential ... I could ask him to play the lead ...

LECTURER I say the Far East because the spleen can be massively enlarged by malaria ...

JANE (*thoughts*) He's getting a grip on them now ... his personality is slowly taking a hold on the shallow striplings ...

FRANCES (*thoughts*) He is so good, why can't we be allowed to enjoy the subject instead of exams, exams all the time.

TERRY (*thoughts*) The lower end of the abdomen ... a Vision of Hell by Heronymous Bosch[3] ... I think the time has come for me to leave the packed benches of cynics and creep down to the front ...

SALLY (*thoughts*) Note for exam: enlargement of the spleen. Note for Rodney: "Book the Squash Court". Note for me: "Get to Family Planning Clinic" ...

MARTIN (*thoughts*) We could do a *revue* ... a revue, that's it ... A mid-term revue to get us over the hump. What could we call it? Hold on to your Scalpels? Bedtime Story? Saturday Night Palsy? ...

TERRY (*thoughts*) They say the bicycle thieves are emptying the racks like mad round here.

MARTIN (*thoughts*) The Sound of Mucus, that's it ... Inspiration in the Anatomy Theatre ... "The Air is Alive, with the Sound of Mucus".

LECTURER (*aloud*) Above the stomach, to the right, is the liver. And under the liver is the gall bladder which stores bile in the digestion of fat. Perhaps with more gall[4] I

1 blood storage organ   2 to vent one's spleen = to express anger
3 late fifteenth-century painter of grotesque surreal fantasies
4 greenish digestive fluid; bold daring.

would be able to make you young persons digest more knowledge.

JARVIS (*thoughts*) Don't say he's going to be funny at this stage.

MARTIN (*thoughts*) Comedian. I'll sign him on to do a sketch ... "I've got sixteen, going on seventeen[1], Babies ..." It's time to think ...

JANE (*thoughts*) He's trying to be human with them ... that won't work.

TERRY (*thoughts*) I wonder if I should make a quick dash for the cycle shed? Say I've been overcome with nausea – no, I can't miss any of this.

FRANCES (*thoughts*) Even the lecturers are trapped in the exam syndrome ... I'll put up a notice in the Concord Building ... to call all students to a meeting to discuss the relevance of the existing exam structures ...

LECTURER (*aloud*) The stomach drains into the duodenum which is wrapped round the head of the pancreas which is another of the digestive glands ... The anatomical relations of this area are complicated and will require further study ...

FRANCES (*thoughts*) I'll go over to the anatomy lab and have a look at those glands ...

MARTIN (*thoughts*) The revue could be in two parts ... Part One ... the Opening Spleen. Part Two ... the Rectus[2] Abdominus. With an interval for drinks and wind ...

TERRY (*thoughts*) God, I hope he's going over this again.

JARVIS (*thoughts*) I do believe old Terry's struggling. I thought he was a nonchalant lad. One of us.

TERRY (*thoughts*) Look at the others, lounging around with various degrees of indifference. I've tried to give the same impression ... it doesn't work ... they can see straight through me ... and what's Martin smiling at?

MARTIN (*thoughts. Sings*) My stomach wants to heave, like the waves on the shore.

JANE (*thoughts*) We all think we're so clever and cynical

---

1 'I am sixteen, going on seventeen' – song from *The Sound of Music* **2** straight muscle

looking down on old Prof . . . but how does he see us?
I wish I could know what he's feeling.

SALLY (*thoughts*) She was on the phone an hour . . . and not
a reference to Dad . . . something's up . . . we need a
few lectures on the phenomena of middle-aged *sex*
life . . .

LECTURER Moving further down the gastro-intestinal tract we
come to the small intestine which is a long
convoluted tube attached to the posterior abdominal
wall . . . It is in this part that the bulk of the
digestion takes place . . .

JARVIS (*thoughts*) Hurry along Prof, I've digested all you
can give me for one morning.

MARTIN (*thoughts*) I'll get Jane in the chorus, with those long
legs that have pre-wrapped many a lusty young
buck.

JANE (*thoughts*) This Prof does things to me that aren't in
any text book . . . and certainly aren't in my
experience.

SALLY (*thoughts*) Dear Mum, I'm sorry to hear about you
and Dad, but with exams so near and me and
Rodney . . .

TERRY (*thoughts*) Dear Father, you may be disappointed to
learn that the Faculty Head has advised me that . . .

MARTIN (*thoughts*) I must get contributory sketches . . . "On
the Right Tracheotomy"[1]. "Top of the Ops"[2] "Great
Expectorations"[3] . . . I'll ask the Prof to
contribute . . .

LECTURER We now reach the large intestine and over in the
right lower quadrant you can see the appendix . . .

TERRY (*thoughts*) Facts, facts, facts . . . how will I
remember them all?

JARVIS (*thoughts*) It seems to me that Terry, after a specific
period of concentration, gives off certain odours of
distress and perplexity . . . That might make a
remarkable study in the biochemistry of stress.

MARTIN (*thoughts*) Beethoven's Abdominal Symphony, that
should make a sketch Prof . . . Andante Appen-
dixe . . .

FRANCES (*thoughts*) If only this lot would stop pretending to be

---

1 removal of windpipe   2 surgical operations   3 coughing up

frivolous; organise a discussion group, debating society ... a forum, instead of each groping blindly on their own ...

LECTURER From the right lower quadrant the colon passes upwards and then across where you will notice the omentum is also attached ...

JARVIS (*thoughts*) This old bean is so pedantic he is incapable of any real discovery. Surprise me Prof.

LECTURER The colon passes down on the left side, here, finally becoming the rectum ...

MARTIN (*thoughts*) The body of the revue will be divided into five parts; the Nasal, the Pharynx[1], the Larynx[2], the Trachea and the Lungs, with the bowels providing the slow movement[3] ...

JARVIS (*thoughts*) Are we nearing the end? Suddenly the hall is bristling with relief as the pack sniffs the closing cadenza[4].

TERRY (*thoughts*) When we finish the heavies down the front will sit concentrating and reading over their notes, while the cynics here at the back will rush for the coffee queue. What shall I do? Be honest and stay, or bluff my way and dash?

SALLY (*thoughts*) I know that Frances runs the Student Help Group ... sits by the telephone to save lives. I wonder if I should talk to her about Mum and Dad?

JANE (*thoughts*) He is systematically concluding ... he has a dignity, a style ... a certain poise ... the eye may be dimming, the muscles may be flagging, the skin may be wrinkling but by God, he makes some of these young hairies look a set of jumped-up monkeys ...

TERRY (*thoughts*) I haven't heard a word of this lecture thinking about my bike ...

LECTURER To round off ...

JARVIS (*thoughts*) OK you've laid it all out, now tell us something to really grab us. I defy you to.

LECTURER I would like to point out an interesting anatomical variation in this patient, which one or two of you may have spotted. No? Then note, there is a little *out*

---

1 throat   **2** voice-box   **3** section of music; passing of excreta   **4** musical flourish *pouching* on the small intestine called Meckel's Diverticulum[1] ...

JARVIS   (*thoughts*) Wow, stun me Prof.

JANE   (*thoughts*) He's won them ... even the cynics have to admit he's pulled it off ... go on Prof ... finish them ...

LECTURER   This is a remnant of the attachment of the yolksac[2] diverticulum, which in Latin means "A Wayside House of Ill Repute". A very satisfactory appellation ... I leave you with the thought, good morning.

(*Applause*)

JARVIS   (*thoughts*) Great Prof ... that's the one I didn't know.

FRANCES   (*thoughts*) Look how they shine when he turns his light on their ignorance ...

JANE   (*thoughts*) Oh, splendid ... splendid ...

MARTIN   (*thoughts*) Curtain line, dah, de dah, that's your lot folks ... (*Aloud*) Hi, Terry, I want to talk to you about a revue.

TERRY   Sorry not my line.

SALLY   Jane, are you coming, or dreaming?

JANE   Get me a coffee and doughnut, I want to sit here for a while.

JARVIS   Bag me a coffee and a Danish Pastry girl. (*Thoughts*) For this lot life is all eating and sleeping, interspersed with prodigious mental efforts.

TERRY   (*thoughts*) Shall I stay here and look over my notes? Or join the mob at the bar.

JARVIS   (*aloud*) Glued to your seat old son?

TERRY   (*aloud*) Am I hell ... race you to the bar ...

JARVIS   (*Thoughts*) There he goes rushing up front to establish his inferiority complex, methinks he has failure in his eyes ...

MARTIN   (*aloud*) I say Frances, don't you think it would be a good idea to put on another revue?

FRANCES   (*aloud*) I think our activities should take on a more serious turn than your flippant revues ... I was

---

1 small bulge in the tube mammals   2 container of fluid on which embryo feeds, not used in mammals

thinking of forming a discussion group on the Exàm Structure ...

MARTIN (*aloud*) Oh ... well I'll come along with you if you come along with me.

FRANCES (*aloud*) It's not who you'll go along with, it's what you believe in ...

SALLY (*aloud*) Frances, you're still on that Students' Lifeline thing, aren't you?

FRANCES Of course I am, why, do you want help?

SALLY Help? Me? That's a laugh. You could always chain up Rodney after squash I suppose ... it does something to the animal in him ...

FRANCES Are you sure you don't want anything?

SALLY Just a coffee and chocolate ... come on.

MARTIN Jane, isn't it about time we did another revue? Could you whip up a chorus again?

JANE I've grown out of showing my legs in public, Martin. You'd better find some first years.

MARTIN God, this lot just need stirring out of their apathy; listen you lot ... about a mid-term revue ... I thought we'd call it The Sound of Mucus.

JARVIS They're not interested, Martin.

MARTIN Don't you think they're all a bit too bloody *intent*, Jarvis?

JARVIS They *are* intent deep down, your revue will only make them forget it for a while ... for the most part they need more drastic surgery.

En Attendant François
by *David Campton*

The Cast

Mavis *an ordinary girl*
Rose *her friend*

After the restaurant meal, the girls go to the Ladies for a chat. On their return they find their escorts have disappeared. They remember the meal and gradually realise that they have been abandoned. The reasons are obvious to the audience but not to the girls.

En Attendant François

A restaurant

Sounds of high heels approaching.

MAVIS Is this our table?

ROSE It's got to be.

MAVIS Why?

ROSE There's nobody sitting at it.

MAVIS That doesn't make it our table, Rose. We can't just park ourselves at any old table because there's nobody sitting at it.

ROSE I recognise this table, Mavis.

MAVIS They all look alike to me.

ROSE I recognise this pink patch where you dropped your beetroot. Look. There.

MAVIS That's not where I dropped my beetroot.

ROSE I recognised it at once.

MAVIS That's where you spilt your wine Rose. *This* is where I dropped my beetroot. I pushed my plate over it.

ROSE Well, if this is where I spilt my wine and that's where you dropped your beetroot, this must be our table.

MAVIS I don't know.

ROSE Mavis! This is where you dropped the beetroot; this is where I spilt the wine; that is where one of them splashed his soup; and that is where the other had an accident with his coffee. It's got to be our table. Ours is the only table where you could frame the cloth and pass it off as modern art.

MAVIS I mean – where are they?

ROSE Surely you don't need me to tell you that. They'll have gone to where we've just been.

MAVIS Are you sure?

ROSE It's natural, isn't it? After all that wine.

MAVIS We didn't see them.

ROSE I should hope not.

MAVIS I mean on the way. Coming or going.

ROSE Where else could they go? It's raining outside. Where do you think they went?

MAVIS I don't know.

ROSE Well, if you can't make a sensible suggestion at least stop asking silly questions and sit down.

They sit.

MAVIS Have you got a headache, Rose?

ROSE Not yet, but I'm working up to it.

MAVIS Somehow I get the feeling that something tonight wasn't quite right in some way.

ROSE You can say that again.

MAVIS I don't think I can. How can I put it –?

ROSE Don't bother.

MAVIS Tonight's night out seemed to lack something that a night out ought to have.

ROSE My fault again, I suppose.

MAVIS You did ask me to come.

ROSE My mistake.

MAVIS You said, "Make up a foursome, Mavis." If you didn't want me, why did you ask me?

ROSE Because you were the first one I thought of.

MAVIS That's nice, Rose. Couldn't you really think of anybody else?

ROSE Why else do you think I asked you?

MAVIS That isn't quite so nice.

ROSE I wasn't trying to be nice. I don't feel like being nice. Not after the way you've jiggered everything.

MAVIS Did I? I didn't mean to jigger anything.

ROSE All you'd got to do was keep yours happy while I ... kept mine happy.

MAVIS You didn't tell me mine could only speak French.

ROSE I wanted it to be a surprise.

MAVIS Rose! You mean you knew all the time he couldn't speak English and didn't tell me?

ROSE Well – surprise is the whole point of a blind date.

MAVIS Oh, it was a surprise all right. The first of many.

ROSE Like I said – you're the only girl I know who can speak French.

MAVIS I can't speak much French.

ROSE I know that now.

MAVIS On the phone you just said "You speak French, don't you?"

ROSE And you said "yes".

MAVIS You didn't ask how much.

ROSE Like I said – my mistake.

MAVIS I thought you'd just want me to read the menu.

ROSE You weren't so hot at that either. "Un portion of cette ici pour moi." I took the Home Economics Course at school, and even I could have said that.

MAVIS Why didn't you?

ROSE Because I never said I could speak French.

MAVIS I never said I could till you asked me.

ROSE My mistake again. I took it for granted that anybody who says they can speak French can speak it better than I can.

MAVIS I never said I could speak French like the French. I can't help it if the French don't speak French the way I was taught.

ROSE The way you speak French ought to be an offence under the Trades Description Act. I don't know what *he* must have been thinking. I can guess, but I don't want to.

MAVIS Oh, I know what he was thinking all right. I wanted to tell him he'd got another thought coming, but I couldn't think of the French for it.

ROSE "Voulez vous promener avec moi?"[1] seemed to mean something to him all right.

MAVIS I hadn't actually meant to say that, but it was all I could think of at the time. It's quite easy to say "voulez vous", but not so easy to find anything to go after it. The words you learn in school don't seem to stretch very far when you're trying to keep up a real conversation. "Est-ce que vous avez écouté le weather forecast" didn't seem to take us very far.

ROSE "Aimez-vous Le Common Market Agricultural Policy" turned out to be a right spanner in the works, too. What do you know about Le Common Agricultural Policy?

MAVIS Nothing. It seemed to set him off, though.

ROSE What was he saying?

MAVIS I didn't know all the words.

ROSE You kept saying "Oui" and "Non".

1 Would you like to walk with me?"

MAVIS That was just to sound intelligent.

ROSE I don't know about intelligent, but you got him worked up all right.

MAVIS In the end I got his general drift. In the end he didn't leave much room for doubt. But that had nothing to do with the Common Market Agricultural Policy.

ROSE The French use their hands a lot. You had to watch his hands.

MAVIS At first I watched them – yes. Then I felt one of them. On my knee.

ROSE Oh. Was that when you dropped your beetroot?

MAVIS No. That was just before I told him to "Arretez[1] that, François". I was smiling at the time because I didn't want to spoil the party. You didn't seem to notice.

ROSE I had enough problems of my own. With all those hands under the table, the waiter must have thought it was an outing for one-armed bandits.

MAVIS After that I had to whisper "Move it". Not in French, of course, because I don't know the French for "Move it" But he understood.

ROSE Did he move it?

MAVIS Yes. *That's* when I dropped my beetroot.

ROSE I noticed that.

MAVIS Yes. That was just before he splashed his soup. When I kicked him.

ROSE You kicked me first.

MAVIS I didn't know your ankles were over my side.

ROSE I didn't know where to put them to keep them out of the way. That's when I spilt my wine.

MAVIS They're taking their time, aren't they?

ROSE Probably examining their bruises.

MAVIS Why? Did you kick yours too?

ROSE He made my coffee go down the wrong way.

MAVIS You made his go all over the table. Lucky they're only little cups.

ROSE You're right, Mavis. Tonight wasn't a very good idea.

MAVIS Oh, I don't know.

ROSE Now don't start contradicting me again, Mavis. If I say it wasn't a very good idea, then it wasn't a very good idea.

MAVIS All right, Rose. It was a lousy idea.

1 stop

ROSE   I didn't say it was a lousy idea. At the time it seemed sort of romantic – like an old black and white movie. Bogart and Bergman[1] stuff. A leap into the unknown and all that.

MAVIS   I was the one doing the leaping, Rose. I was the one stuck with the blind date.

ROSE   I'd only met mine once before.

MAVIS   Rose! You mean you agreed to this – this – when you'd only met the man once?

ROSE   Well, you agreed and you hadn't met yours at all.

MAVIS   I trusted you, Rose. How could you?

ROSE   Easy. Mine's a rep[2].

MAVIS   A rep!?

ROSE   Don't sound like that. Yours might be a rep, too, if only we knew.

MAVIS   You didn't tell me he was a rep.

ROSE   You didn't ask.

MAVIS   A rep! I know reps. Them and their sample cases.

ROSE   I didn't ask what he'd got in this sample case. We just got to chatting ... you know the way you do. He said, "Shall we?" I said, "I don't mind." And he said, "I don't suppose you've got a friend who speaks French."

MAVIS   Why should he want to know if you'd got a friend who speaks French?

ROSE   Because he's got a friend who speaks French.

MAVIS   How do you know?

ROSE   You heard him. At least it sounded like French coming from him.

MAVIS   I don't think we speak the same language.

ROSE   That's obvious ... They're a long time coming back.

MAVIS   The longer the better for me. What must be on their minds?

ROSE   You know perfectly well what's on their minds. What's been there all night.

MAVIS   They're mistaken. At least they're mistaken about me. I only hope they're mistaken about you, Rose.

ROSE   Of course they're mistaken ... What exactly did you mean by that?

MAVIS   You're full of surprises, Rose.

---

1 famous early film stars Humphrey Bogart and Ingrid Bergman   **2** representative, travelling salesperson

ROSE   I wasn't the one who ordered hors d'oeuvres.

MAVIS I only ordered hors d'oeuvres because it sounded French.
       I wanted him to feel at home. I didn't expect it to include
       bits of beetroot. I didn't expect him to order tomato
       soup.

ROSE   Perhaps he wanted to make you feel at home.

MAVIS He went a funny way about it.

ROSE   Just think – if you'd both ordered prawn cocktail we
       might still have a clean cloth.

MAVIS Not after your wine and his coffee.

ROSE   He needed that coffee too. After all that wine . . . It looks
       like a map of somewhere.

MAVIS Well? Where do we go from here?

ROSE   Go?

MAVIS Go, Rose. Go.

ROSE   You mean – go?

MAVIS We could.

ROSE   Before they come back?

MAVIS It would serve them right. Treating us like – well – what
       they were treating us like.

ROSE   They're quite well mannered really. They say "please"
       and "thank you".

MAVIS I haven't heard them saying "please" and "thank you".

ROSE   Actions speak louder.

MAVIS In that case they've been saying "please" all night. Are
       we going to wait for them to say "thank you"?

ROSE   That depends on what they're saying "thank you" for.

MAVIS There's only one thing they want to say "thank you" for.

ROSE   We ought not to forget our manners. We really ought to
       stay and say "thank you".

MAVIS For what?

ROSE   For the meal of course.

MAVIS If we stay to say "thank you" for that, we'll end by
       saying "thank you" for the other. That's what they're
       expecting. If you will go round chatting up reps what can
       you expect? Once they get back here they'll cut off our
       retreat.

ROSE   Let's think about it.

MAVIS We haven't got much longer.

ROSE   Consider all the angles.

MAVIS We were out there for over a quarter of an hour
       ourselves, repairing the ravages.

ROSE   Only the ordinary ravages after a dinner out. Lipstick and powder and the ladder in your tights.

MAVIS   They're bound to be back any minute. Any second.

ROSE   Don't rush me.

MAVIS   You don't want to go, do you, Rose? You want to stay. You want . . .

ROSE   I want to do the right thing. It doesn't seem fair to run out on them. I've got a soft spot.

MAVIS   Guess where.

ROSE   Besides, it's raining and they've got the car. If we ditch them, who's going to drive us home?

MAVIS   If we can't trust them at a table in full view, how can we trust them in a lay-by?

ROSE   Who said anything about a lay-by?

MAVIS   You know what a lay-by is.

ROSE   I know what it's not going to be. They've merely got the wrong idea about us, Mavis. That's all. We'll just have to put them right and not rouse their expectations.

MAVIS   Their expectations are roused already. Their roused expectations could be the reason why they're such a long time coming back. They are probably still in there comparing their expectations. Their expectations could be right up there – sky high.

ROSE   Well, their expectations will just have to come down again. We must make sure of that.

MAVIS   How?

ROSE   Talk to them gently but firmly. I'll talk to mine. You talk to yours.

MAVIS   In French?

ROSE   He'll get the idea.

MAVIS   Vous avez le wrong idea. What's French for wrong idea?

ROSE   Don't ask me. I told you – I took Home Economics. I can tell you what to do if your bread isn't rising fast enough.

MAVIS   Rising bread is not my particular problem à ce moment. Je suis une jeune fille très respectable.

ROSE   What about me?

MAVIS   Et mon ami est très respectable aussi. Nous sommes only ici pour le diner. How does that sound?

ROSE   Grim.

MAVIS   I'm doing my best without a dictionary. If only you'd warned me, I'd have brought my phrase book. Je suis trying to be tactful. It is difficile enough saying "think again" in English. In French it's practically impossible.

ROSE Pensez encore?

MAVIS Eh?

ROSE Pensez encore. Think again.

MAVIS If I were you, I'd stick to Home Economics. We've got to break it gently. Er – nous le fracassons doucement.

ROSE It might be easier just to give in gracefully.

MAVIS Rose – I cannot speak for you, but personally I am not giving in for want of the right word.

ROSE Le mot juste. I know that one.

MAVIS It's not the one I was looking for. Je still cherche le mot. Je suis un peu rusty, that's all.

ROSE Rusty? You're practically siezed up. By the time you've found the right word you'll both be singing The Marseillaise[1].

MAVIS Then the mot juste est "non". Non – parlé avec tout conviction.

ROSE Is "non" going to be enough, Mavis?

MAVIS It is if followed by a smack dans ses yeux avec mon portmanteau[2].

ROSE You haven't brought a portmanteau.

MAVIS With my handbag, then.

ROSE It all sounds a bit undignified, somehow.

MAVIS Seulement as a dernier resort. First je intend to appeal a son better nature.

ROSE Bon.

MAVIS Oui, bon.

ROSE Mind you, apres tout ces bottles of beaujolais je wouldn't rely on the better nature of this pair.

MAVIS Now I wish I'd taken the Home Economics Course.

ROSE How would a Home Economics Course help in this situation?

MAVIS It wouldn't. But at least I shouldn't be expected to talk French while I'm fighting off a drunken sex maniac.

ROSE What's French for sex maniac?

MAVIS Mayday.

ROSE Mayday?

MAVIS You shout it.

ROSE Vous avez un point.

---

1 French National song **2** travelling trunk

MAVIS Only shouting "mayday"[1] won't do me much good if you're fighting off yours at the same time.

ROSE At least I can say "Lay off, Buster" to mine.

MAVIS Say it for me, too. Perhaps he can translate.

ROSE Right. As soon as they come back.

MAVIS If they *are* coming back.

ROSE Eh? Don't be ... Mavis! You don't think –?

MAVIS Just a thought.

ROSE I wish you wouldn't.

MAVIS Over a quarter of an hour. Nearly half if they went just before we started back.

ROSE They wouldn't ...

MAVIS What have they got to come back for?

ROSE Us.

MAVIS Big deal.

ROSE They've got to come back.

MAVIS Of course, Rose. They've got to come back. If only to pay the bill.

ROSE The bill?

MAVIS The bill. L'addition.

Slight pause.

ROSE Oh, God!

MAVIS Mon Dieu.

ROSE They wouldn't leave us to pay the bill.

MAVIS We're here. Where are they?

ROSE In the mens.

MAVIS All this time?

ROSE They've got to be in the mens.

MAVIS What could they be doing in the mens all the time?

ROSE How should I know what men get up to in the mens?

MAVIS You know more than me about things like that. You've had more experience.

ROSE Thank you very much. For your information my experience has never stretched to being with a man in the mens. Neither by accident nor invitation.

MAVIS Only a suggestion.

ROSE Will you stop suggesting? You suggested they may have left us stranded.

---

1 "m'aidez" – "help me", the international distress call

MAVIS I didn't say they had. Only that they might have done.

ROSE Why should they leave us stranded?

MAVIS We did kick them.

ROSE I didn't kick mine very hard.

MAVIS Nor me. Just enough to convey that some things are not wanted here.

ROSE But *he's* wanted here. One of them anyway. Right now. Before the bill comes. If not ... How much have you got in your handbag?

MAVIS Only enough for an emergency.

ROSE Enough for –?

MAVIS I always keep enough for an emergency.

ROSE Why didn't you say so sooner. Letting me sit here in a cold sweat. As long as we've got enough for an emergency ...

MAVIS But this isn't an emergency, Rose. This is a disaster. I haven't got enough for a disaster. Only about enough for the bus. If the buses haven't stopped running.

ROSE They will have done by the time we've stopped explaining to the manager.

MAVIS And washing up.

ROSE Washing up? Oh, no! Not in this get-up. ... They might still be in the mens.

MAVIS Do you think so?

ROSE No.

MAVIS What can we do now?

ROSE Well, we could call for the manager.

MAVIS I don't think much of that idea.

ROSE Or we could wait till the manager comes to us.

MAVIS I don't think much of that, either.

ROSE What else can we do?

MAVIS Run?

ROSE After all that wine?

MAVIS Is there any left?

ROSE Surely you don't want any more. You'll be sliding under the table.

MAVIS Better than running up the wall.

ROSE (*holding up the bottle*) Here.

MAVIS Look.

ROSE A couple of centimetres at the bottom.

MAVIS Under the bottle.

ROSE The bill!

MAVIS Don't touch it. Don't read it. Don't tell me. I don't want to know. How much?

ROSE It's been paid.

MAVIS Paid?

ROSE There's a message. On the back. In French. What does it mean?

MAVIS (*after a quick glance*) Goodbye. Sort of.

ROSE Like au revoir.

MAVIS Except au revoir means hope to see you again and – this – means hope we don't.

ROSE They're certainly no gentlemen, leaving a message like that where anybody could read it.

MAVIS They're no gentlemen, leaving us.

ROSE They didn't know you were thinking of shouting "mayday".

MAVIS I wouldn't have shouted very loud.

ROSE I'd probably have been too occupied to hear you anyway.

MAVIS It's still raining.

ROSE The last bus goes in two minutes.

MAVIS So what we do now?

ROSE There's only one thing we can do.

BOTH Run.

Which they do.

Nightmare
by *R. D. Wingfield*

The Cast

Thorpe *a police inspector*
Drew *a police constable*
Radio *voice over police radio*
Announcer *voice on domestic radio*
Woman *staying in the cottage (small part)*
Drummond *middle-aged man having the nightmare*
Smith *the mysterious intruder*

The police are hunting an escaped psychopath from the hospital during a storm. He seems to be making for an isolated cottage, with a stolen car and a lethal knife. Drummond wakes to hear the woman in the cottage screaming, and to relive his nightmare yet again.

Recorded sound effects are necessary for performance.

Nightmare

1 A country road at night

Torrential rain, crash of thunder.
A police car, siren wailing, approaches at speed then skids to a halt.

THORPE You nearly had me through the windscreen, Drew. What's up?

DREW There's a fallen tree blocking the road, sir ... it'll take a crane to shift it.

THORPE Damn ... can we detour?

DREW The side roads are flooded ...

RADIO (*distort*) Control to Inspector Thorpe ... Control to Inspector Thorpe ...

A handset is picked up.

THORPE Thorpe.

RADIO The hospital's just phoned sir. One of the doctors' cars is missing. Clayton must have taken it.

THORPE Blast ... So he's got a car and he's got a knife ... We're stuck on the Belford Road ... the storm's brought a ruddy great tree down. Clayton's bound to be making for the cottage. Have you been able to warn the Occupier?

RADIO Not yet, sir ... the phone wires are down.

THORPE Right ... get a crane down here right away to shift this tree, then send a couple of cars on to the cottage ... Drew and I will try and get there on foot. Are the BBC putting out the News Flash?

RADIO Should be going out any time now, sir.

THORPE It's nearly midnight ... let's hope someone's still up to listen to it ... he's killed once ... we don't want to give him a second chance ...

2 Cottage Kitchen

Quick crossfade to interior of cottage kitchen. Outside the storm is raging. The woman occupant is washing up. Sound of running water; clatter of crockery; music from radio which crackles from the effects of the storm. As she works she hums the tune being played on the radio. Music fades.

ANNOUNCER We interrupt our programme of late night music for an urgent Police Message. Householders in the Renwick area warned to be on the look-out for Henry John Clayton who escaped earlier this evening from the maximum security wing of Ranford Hospital after stabbing a male nurse. Clayton, who is serving a life sentence for the murder of his wife, is aged 49, sallow complexion, dark hair, medium build. The Police stress that Clayton is dangerous and on no account should be approached ... If seen, inform the Police immediately. Keep doors and windows locked.

While the News Flash is being read, the woman at first stops washing up to listen, but after a while loses interest and resumes the washing up, humming the dance tune she has just heard. She is clearly not listening to the Announcer. In the background we hear the tinkling of glass from a smashed window. The woman apparently does not hear this and carries on as before ... Then there is the sound, off, of an open window banging in the wind. She stops ...

WOMAN What ...? (*Listening*) Sounds like the lounge window ...

She sighs with annoyance. Turns off tap, crosses kitchen and opens the door ... she gasps ...

Who are you? ... How did you get in ...? No! ... please ... No! ... (*Screams*)

Thud as she falls to the floor.

ANNOUNCER ... We now return you to your late night dance music ...

Cheerful music ... Fade.

3 The upstairs bedroom of the cottage

Alarm clock ticking. Sounds of storm from outside. Windows banging from downstairs. Heavy breathing from sleeping man who sighs and moans restlessly in his sleep as if in the throes of a nightmare. Through the wind and the rain, gradually becoming louder as it impinges into the man's consciousness, comes the scream and pleadings from the woman in the kitchen – but on slight distort.

WOMAN No ... please ... no! (*Screams*)

Allow the scream to linger until abruptly cut off. Drummond awakes with a start and sits up in bed.

DRUMMOND What was that?
He listens, panting with fright ... but there is now only the sounds of the wind and the rain ... he sighs with relief.
A nightmare! But it sounded so real ... like Joan's voice ... (*With a start he realises his wife is not in bed beside him*) Joan!!

Thunder rumbles overhead.

Oh ... she'll be sleeping with the kids.

Picks up alarm clock.

Almost midnight ... what's that?

He becomes aware of the banging of the downstairs window.

A window open ... Damn!

Creak of springs as he gets out of bed.

Better go and see to it ...

Light switch on and off.

Blast! Should be a torch somewhere.

Rattle of bedside drawer.

Ah! *Torch switched on.*
Now then ...

Footsteps across room. Door opens. Footsteps along passage, down stairs. Window banging violently in the wind gets closer. Footsteps across wooden floor. Door opens.

What the . . . ! Who the hell are you?

Clap of thunder from above.

4 Outside

Quick crossfade to exterior. Torrential rain . . . the Inspector and the Constable struggling on foot.

THORPE Come on, Constable.

DREW *(panting)* I'm doing the best I can, sir. Reckon we could take a short cut across the field.

THORPE The rain's turned it into a quagmire[1]. We'd be up to our knees . . . we'll have to stick to the paths, but hurry . . .

Thunder as before.

5 Cottage kitchen

SMITH Did I frighten you? I'm terribly sorry . . . I didn't realise there was anyone in the house.

DRUMMOND I bet you didn't . . . keep still!!

SMITH Please . . . I don't like lights shining in my eyes.

DRUMMOND And I don't like people breaking into my house . . . Stand there . . . by the wall.

Picks up phone.

SMITH What are you going to do?

DRUMMOND I'm phoning the Police.

Jiggles receiver rest.

SMITH It's not working, I'm afraid.

DRUMMOND How do you know?

SMITH I tried it when I came in. I imagine the storm's brought the wires down.

Drummond replaces phone.

Perhaps you'd let me explain?

DRUMMOND Shut up! What's in that bag?

SMITH Bag?

1 boggy dangerous marsh

48

DRUMMOND Come on ... what have you stolen?

SMITH Oh no ... I haven't stolen anything. This is my stuff.

Clicks bag open.

Look ... bandages ... drugs ... I'm a doctor.

DRUMMOND A doctor?

SMITH From the hospital ... my car's in a ditch a couple of miles from here ... I just skidded ... I was out on a call.

DRUMMOND If you broke down a couple of miles away, why come here?

SMITH Where else was there? You're the only place for miles. I've been hammering and banging at your front door.

DRUMMOND I didn't hear you.

A roll of thunder overhead.

SMITH I'm not surprised with that competition. Anyway, I knocked, there was no reply so I'm afraid I wrongly assumed the cottage was empty ... sorry about your window ... I'll pay for the damage, of course.

DRUMMOND Who were you going to phone?

SMITH The hospital to let them know what had happened, and a garage to pick up my car. Could you trust me enough now to stop blinding me with that torch?

DRUMMOND Sorry.

SMITH That's better ... but you had every right to be careful ... I was alarmed myself when I heard the News Flash.

DRUMMOND What News Flash?

SMITH Oh! ... Nothing ... It was all a bit vague ...

He removes his mac.

You've got a charming place here, Mr ...?

DRUMMOND The name's Drummond ... John Drummond ... and it isn't mine ... I've only rented it ... we're here on holiday.

SMITH A holiday! Dear, dear, we're not obliging you with decent weather, are we?

Rain louder.

49

Just listen to it ...

He moves to a window.

I say, I really made a mess of your window, didn't I? There's a nasty sliver of glass on the carpet. You could stab someone to death with this.

DRUMMOND Put it in the ashtray.

Sound of glass dropped in ashtray.

I don't think you told me what *your* name was?

SMITH Didn't I? It's Smith ... Dr John Smith ... of hotel register fame ... What are you staring at?

DRUMMOND You've got blood all over your sleeve.

SMITH Where? ... Oh! So I have.

DRUMMOND You've gashed your wrist.

SMITH From the window, I suppose ... How clumsy of me.

DRUMMOND You'll need a plaster ... there's a First Aid box in the kitchen.

SMITH (*sharply*) No! (*Milder*) No ... please don't bother going into the kitchen ...

Opens bag and rummages.

I've got plasters here somewhere ... Ah.

Tears cover from plaster and sticks to wound.

There ... Physician heal thyself![1]

DRUMMOND Seemed a lot of blood for such a tiny cut.

SMITH Who'd have thought the old man had so much blood in him?[2] (*Suddenly and sharply*) Please put that down!

DRUMMOND I was just looking.

SMITH I'd like the knife back please ... thank you.

Drops knife in bag and clicks shut.

I don't allow anyone to go through my bag.

DRUMMOND I'm sorry.

SMITH No ... it's me who should apologise ... I break into your house ... I smash your window. It's just

---

1 Bible: *Luke* I iii 23   **2** 'Yet who would have thought the old man to have had so much blood in him' – Shakespeare: *Macbeth* V i 40

that I've had drugs stolen ... Not that I'm suggesting ...

DRUMMOND I thought I'd seen that knife before. We have one like it in the kitchen.

SMITH Oh no ... this is hospital issue, I assure you ... but they're very common and very sharp ... I always carry one ... it's surprising the uses one finds for a sharp knife. I ought to be on my way I suppose.

Roll of thunder.

DRUMMOND You're not going out in this.

SMITH They'll be worrying about me at the hospital.

DRUMMOND Then they'll have to worry ... you'd never make it back in this anyway. You must stay here.

SMITH My dear Mr Drummond I wouldn't dream of putting you to such trouble.

DRUMMOND No trouble ... This settee opens out into a bed. I'll have to wake my wife ... she'll know where the spare bedclothes are.

SMITH Your wife! No ... please don't disturb her ... she must be sleeping very soundly. If I could just sit in this chair ... (*sits*) That's better ...

DRUMMOND I don't think I could get back to sleep anyway. I had this nightmare ... a woman screaming ... it sounded so real.

SMITH [The awful thing about nightmares is that they sometimes go on after you've woken up ... this cottage holds such terrible memories.

DRUMMOND What do you mean?

SMITH Oh ... it's all ancient history ... a long time ago ... You wouldn't be interested.

DRUMMOND You always get stories about these old places.

SMITH Of course you do.]

Drummond yawns.

You're tired and I'm keeping you up. It's too bad of me ... Go on ... up you go ... I'll be all right.

DRUMMOND I couldn't sleep.

SMITH Then let the Doctor prescribe a sedative ...

He opens bag.
Here ...

DRUMMOND	No thanks ... I've swallowed enough pills in my time to sink a battleship. (*Yawns again*) I think I'll make myself some coffee ... would you like a cup?

Smith jumps from chair and moving to kitchen door ...

SMITH	No!
DRUMMOND	[What are you playing at? Do you mind moving away from the kitchen door. (*Pause*) Do you mind moving I said ... I want to get past.
SMITH	It's best you don't go in there.
DRUMMOND	What the hell are you talking about? Why shouldn't I go into my own kitchen?
SMITH	That News Flash ... It was about a dangerous patient who'd escaped from Ranford Hospital.
DRUMMOND	So?
SMITH	He's been here.]
DRUMMOND	What ...?
SMITH	I wanted to spare you.
DRUMMOND	Spare me what for God's sake?
SMITH	I found her when I broke in ...
DRUMMOND	Get out of my way!

Shoves Smith to one side and opens kitchen door.

	I wish the blessed lights were working. (*Gasps*) Joan!!
SMITH	(*gently*) I wouldn't touch her if I were you.
DRUMMOND	You're a doctor ... can't you do something?
SMITH	Believe me, Mr Drummond, I've done everything I can ...
	Clap of thunder.

6 Outside again

Raining hard, Inspector Thorpe is panting. He has fallen behind PC Drew.

DREW	(*calls*) Inspector!
THORPE	What?
DREW	Over here, sir ... the car.
THORPE	(*approaching*) So he's abandoned it ... why?

Drew opens car door.

DREW	Perhaps he ran out of petrol.
THORPE	Any sign of the knife?

DREW   (*rummaging*) Not immediately apparent, sir.

THORPE   Then he's taken it to the cottage with him. Come on ... let's hope we can get there before he uses it ...

7 Cottage lounge

Crossfade to interior of cottage. Spoon chinking in glass as liquid is stirred.

SMITH   Here ... drink this ...

DRUMMOND   What is it?

SMITH   A mild sedative ... Come on ... you're shaking like a leaf.

DRUMMOND   I heard her scream ... I thought it was a nightmare ... if only I'd gone down straight away.

SMITH   Do you have a car?

DRUMMOND   Yes ... why?

SMITH   I think I'd better go and get the Police.

DRUMMOND   In the garage ... I'll wait here.

SMITH   Take the sedative first.

DRUMMOND   I've got to keep awake ... I must go and see if the children are all right.

SMITH   (*sharply*) Children? There are children here?

DRUMMOND   I must go to them.

SMITH   You're in no state to go anywhere. I'll go and see if they're all right. Where are they?

DRUMMOND   Upstairs ... the room above this.

SMITH   I'll take the torch.

[*Opens and closes bag.*

DRUMMOND   What did you take from your bag?

SMITH   Nothing.

DRUMMOND   You took something out ... I saw you.

SMITH   I put the sedative packet back ... I took nothing out.

DRUMMOND   What's that in your hand? Show me? What are you going to do with that knife?]

8 Outside the cottage

Rain ... Inspector Thorpe and PC Drew's running footsteps through undergrowth. They are panting heavily and gasping for breath.

DREW   Is it much further, sir?

THORPE   No ... we're here ... That's Forest View Cottage. Quietly now ...

They approach.

DREW   Look ... a broken window.

THORPE   Give me a couple of seconds to get to the front door, then kick the rest of it in.

Sounds of a struggle and yell of pain from within.

No time. Come on!

Sound of the window kicked in as Thorpe and Drew burst into lounge.

All right hold it you two ... We're Police Officers.

Struggle stops.

DRUMMOND   He's got a knife.

DREW   Give it to me!

SMITH   All right ... but stop shining that torch in my eyes.

DREW   Who are you? You first.

SMITH   The name's Smith ... Dr John Smith.

DRUMMOND   He's not a doctor ... He's the escaped prisoner you're looking for ... He killed my wife ...

THORPE   What??

DRUMMOND   In the kitchen ...

He opens door to kitchen.

THORPE   Dear God! Drew ... radio for an ambulance ... and a doctor.

SMITH   But I am a doctor ... Look ...

Rustle of papers.

My identification ... driving licence ... hospital pass. This is Clayton!

[DRUMMOND   What are you talking about? My name's Drummond ... I'm here on holiday with my wife and children.

SMITH   Would you take a look upstairs, Constable. He claims there are two children up there.

DREW   Right.

His footsteps fade away upstairs and are heard overhead during the next speeches.

DRUMMOND   What do you mean I "claim" there are two children up there ... there are two children ... my children ...

SMITH   Mr Drummond ... do you know the date?

DRUMMOND   Of course I do ... July 15th.

SMITH   And the year ...?

DRUMMOND   1959!

SMITH   (*gently*) It's 1979.]

DRUMMOND   What are you talking about?

SMITH   And the woman in the kitchen isn't your wife ... your wife's been dead a long time ... you killed her twenty years ago.

During the above PC Drew returns.

THORPE   Well, Constable?

DREW   Two little kids sir ... both fast asleep ... a boy of about six ... a girl about eight.

DRUMMOND   You see ... my children ...

SMITH   Your children are married with kids of their own, Mr Drummond.

THORPE   Wait a minute ... "Drummond" ... that's the name Clayton used when he rented this cottage in 1959.

SMITH   His last holiday with his wife and kids. He'd embezzled £20,000 from his farm and he knew the Police were looking for him ... His mind gave way under the strain ... he killed his wife, then he tried to kill himself, but he bungled it.

DRUMMOND   I never touched the children.

SMITH   Of course you didn't Mr Clayton, of course you didn't.

DRUMMOND   You're Dr Smith, aren't you? ... From the hospital ...?

SMITH   That's right ... we have long chats, don't we? When I heard you'd ... run away ... I thought you'd come back here ... where it all began.

THORPE   What about the woman in the kitchen?

SMITH   She's all right ... when Clayton burst in on her she must have fainted ... hit her head on the floor ...

mild concussion, nothing more ... We'll get her to the hospital for a check-up, but I don't think there's much harm done.

DRUMMOND There was blood all over her.

SMITH No Mr Clayton ... there was no blood. There was twenty years ago, but not now ... the nightmare just keeps going on and on I'm afraid ...

Sound of approaching police siren outside.

THORPE At last ... get them to radio through for an ambulance.

DREW Right sir. (*Goes*)

SMITH Come on Mr Clayton. Let's get back. Do you know, I believe it's actually stopped raining ...

Bring up sound of the approaching police car and fade.

The En Suite Bathroom

by *William Humble*

The Cast

Helen *Alan's irritatingly honest wife*
Joe *the friendly plumber*
Alan *a newly-appointed comprehensive headmaster*

Helen warms to the delightfully easy-going workman, while Alan feels it his duty to keep the "working classes" firmly in their place. Unfortunately, classes and standards have changed, and Alan's snobbery only causes him discomfort and embarrassment in this amusingly exaggerated little moral tale.

The En Suite Bathroom

1 A bedroom

Sound of door opening.

HELEN It's in here, Mr ... er ...

JOE Joe.

HELEN Yes. Joe ... My husband – Alan – and I have been wondering what to do with it ever since we moved here ... Then we suddenly thought – well it is next to our room – the obvious thing's an en suite[1] bathroom! Didn't we, darling?

ALAN Well all our friends say they don't know what they ever did without one.

HELEN Not that we let ourselves be affected by that sort of thing.

ALAN Certainly not!

HELEN I mean we didn't get a deep-freeze till *ages* after everyone else.

ALAN Months!

HELEN Well not months, darling ... Not actually months.

ALAN It seemed like months ...

HELEN *Anyway* – what do you think, Mr – er – Joe?

JOE Oh yeah – well I'm all for them.

ALAN (*chuckling*) Yes well you would be, wouldn't you? Honestly darling – what a question!

HELEN (*a bit tight-lipped*) What I meant was, do you think it would be possible? In here?

JOE 'Tis a bit poky ...

HELEN There you are! You see darling.

JOE Still, I suppose you could put in a hip-bath – you know, stick it in the corner over there. Very popular they are.

HELEN Oh, I like that idea ... don't you? I wouldn't mind that at all!

[1] attached (opening off the bathroom)

ALAN (*cool*) You have what you want, darling.

JOE What colour?

HELEN Can't we get a chart or something? What do *you* think?

JOE I'd have thought avocado'd be your sort of colour . . .

HELEN Oh I like that, yes! Avocado! Don't you think, darling?

ALAN Well actually I'm not . . .

JOE You can pop round and look at ours if you want.

ALAN (*even less enthusiastic*) Your bathroom's avocado, is it?

JOE Our en suite bathroom, yeah.

ALAN (*reeling a bit*) You've got an en suite bathroom?

HELEN (*making light of it*) Of course he has! A perk of the job. Like teachers having an endless supply of stationery!

ALAN (*a bit tight*) That's not true, darling. You know perfectly well –

JOE You a teacher, are you?

ALAN (*sharply*) No.

HELEN No, Alan's a headmaster.

ALAN Darling . . .

HELEN Just been appointed. As a matter of fact he's the youngest headmaster in the area.

ALAN (*hastily*) I'm sure Joe doesn't want to –

HELEN Don't be so modest darling! . . . He's terribly busy, you see. I mean up till now we've *always* done this sort of thing ourselves – wouldn't have dreamt of getting anyone in – but I suppose if one can afford it . . .

ALAN Please darling . . .

HELEN And really there just isn't the time.

JOE Too many parents' evenings, eh?

HELEN We do have to do rather a lot of entertaining, as a matter of fact.

JOE Yeah – I saw your barbecue on the patio . . .

ALAN (*interrupting – defiantly*) Anyway – I'm afraid I prefer cream.

HELEN What?

ALAN To avocado. More subtle. No offence meant.

JOE What school is it?

ALAN Sparkdale Comprehensive. (*Still trying to force the conversation back*) And we'll want matching toilet, washbasin and bath – all very plain and simple ... .

JOE (*to himself*) Sparkdale Comprehensive . . .

ALAN (*distracted*) You know it, do you?

JOE (*meaningfully*) Do I know it . . .

HELEN	Of course he knows it, darling. I mean you do live round here, Mr ... don't you, Joe?
JOE	Yeah. Right load of yobs, they are.
ALAN	(*the Headmaster routine taking over*) Ah – so you're in our catchment area. Do you have any children yourself?
JOE	Just the one.
ALAN	What age?
JOE	Twelve.
ALAN	Then I suppose he goes to Sparkdale? I don't remember meeting him – but I have only just started – so many to get to know –
JOE	Not likely. He goes to the prep school down the road.
ALAN	(*shocked*) Palmers Hall?
JOE	That's it.
HELEN	Goodness ...
JOE	You know – nice uniforms.
ALAN	Yes. They – er – that is – we don't believe in uniforms at Sparkdale.
HELEN	(*shocked*) It is rather expensive, isn't it?
JOE	I want him to have the best education he can get.
HELEN	(*on the defensive*) They do say Sparkdale –
ALAN	No no – it's a free country, darling. I'd be the last person to say Sparkdale's perfect ...
HELEN	But you have only been there three weeks, haven't you?
ALAN	(*irritated*) Do be quiet darling.
JOE	I'll – er – go and get the catalogue ...
ALAN	Eh?
JOE	(*going*) It's in the car ...

Sound of bathroom door shutting.

HELEN	(*heatedly*) I'd appreciate it if you didn't talk to me like that in front of other people, Alan.
ALAN	Well really – cheap little jibes[1] about pinching the school stationery ...
HELEN	Just because he annoyed you.
ALAN	How on earth a man like that can afford to send his child to private school ...
HELEN	Well you wouldn't want to, would you?
ALAN	Good God no!
HELEN	Well then.

1 mocking insults

ALAN I'm not saying that! I believe wholeheartedly in the state system. One hundred per cent.

HELEN And it would look a bit off, not sending your own children to your own school.

ALAN Exactly.

HELEN I shouldn't worry then.

ALAN I'm not worrying! All I'm saying is, we couldn't possibly afford to send our kids to private school even if we wanted – heaven forbid ... And while I'm all for the manual worker getting his fair whack – I mean I have always said that, haven't I?

HELEN You have darling, yes.

ALAN I mean I don't think anyone could accuse me of being reactionary[1] ... but one ought to get *some* recognition for a good education and a responsible position! That's not asking too much, surely?!

Sound of bathroom door being opened. An abrupt change of tone from Alan ...

Ah, Joe! That was quick ...

JOE There's the different colours ...

Pages of a catalogue being turned.

And that's the hip-bath. See?

ALAN Hmm ... Tell me – do you have one of these yourself?

JOE Yeah. In the spare bedroom.

ALAN (*a little victory*) You know, I don't think we will have one after all.

Commence fade.

I think we'll plump for the good old-fashioned traditional sort ...

2 Downstairs

Banging from upstairs.

ALAN Does he have to make that awful noise?

HELEN He can hardly be expected to do major plumbing work in total silence, darling.

ALAN God knows how we're going to pay him ...

---

1 against social change

HELEN I thought they'd upped your scale[1] or whatever it is, since you became headmaster.

ALAN (*patiently*) Yes but they've also upped my tax.

HELEN That's no problem, surely, darling – I mean since we increased the mortgage anyway to pay for the fitted kitchen – well surely that means you'll get more tax relief on it?

ALAN But it also means I shall have to pay more mortgage in the first place, darling.

HELEN (*dismayed*) You mean you won't actually gain anything?

ALAN Let's say I shan't lose quite so much.

HELEN That's dreadful darling. I never realised . . .

ALAN (*a weary sigh*) And then of course there's last year's summer holiday.

HELEN Last year's?!! What about this year's?

ALAN (*groaning*) Don't talk to me about this year's.

HELEN Joe tells me he's renting a little villa in the Dordogne[2].

ALAN (*viciously*) And don't talk to me about Joe.

HELEN I don't know how he does it.

ALAN (*darkly*) I do.

The blaring of a transistor radio combining with the banging from upstairs.

HELEN He seems a very easy-going sort of man. Not a care in the world. And yet he's got all these financial commitments. I don't know how he does it . . .

ALAN It's called tax evasion.

HELEN (*shocked*) Darling!

ALAN Don't talk to me about self-employed . . .

HELEN I wasn't.

ALAN They're all the same – one massive tax fiddle. I bet he doesn't declare half of what he earns. "You don't mind paying in cash, do you? Saves all the paperwork." Frankly, you know it sickens me!

HELEN That's jealousy, darling.

ALAN It is not – it's immoral, that's what it is. We're paying for his sort, you know – our taxes go in his pocket!

HELEN Well not entirely . . .

ALAN What do you mean by that?

---

1 put you on a higher rate of pay **2** area of central southern France

HELEN Well you didn't declare the money you got from that article in the Guardian Educational Section, darling.

ALAN   That's entirely different.

HELEN The one on teaching children to use their initiative.

ALAN   I know the one you mean! Anyway that was just a few pounds ... you can't compare ...

HELEN (*soothing*) I'm sure you're right, darling.

ALAN   (*rebelliously*) One thing's for certain. *I'm* not taking part in any under-the-counter hole-in-the-corner deals ... none of this paying by cash to make it simpler. As far as I'm concerned it's all completely fair and above-board. He can have the money by cheque or not at all. That'll fix him!

3 Next day

HELEN It's beautiful – you've done a beautiful job, Joe ... hasn't he darling? ... Darling – what are you doing?

Grunts from Alan.

ALAN   Isn't this washbasin rather shaky?

JOE   Yeah well it will wobble if you jerk it about before the cement's dried. I did warn you.

ALAN   I don't think you did.

HELEN He did darling. I definitely remember.

ALAN   (*ratty*) Oh, well ... I couldn't have heard. Sorry ...

HELEN And I do think the avocado's much better than the cream. So *boring* cream ... Don't you think, darling?

ALAN   Yes, well, you can hardly expect me to agree as I did specifically ask for cream ... Still I suppose I can't really expect any notice to be taken of my wishes ... After all, I'm only paying the bills, when all's said and done ...

JOE   Oh yeah – payment.

ALAN   (*muttering*) I thought *that*'d make you prick your ears up.

JOE   Eh?

ALAN   I'm afraid I've got a bit of a nasty shock for you, Joe. Contrary to what I believe is normal practice in the dubious world of the self-employed ...

HELEN (*horrified*) Darling ...

ALAN   I do not intend to cross your palm with silver, or even with paper money, in fact I do not conspire with you to cheat the Inland Revenue in any way at all.

JOE Do you know what he's on about?

HELEN (*nervously*) Yes it's perfectly simple . . .

ALAN (*ploughing on*) More than that – more than wishing to protect the Inland Revenue, an organisation for whom I have no particular liking – I'm making my stand to protect the ordinary, decent, thirty-p-in-the-pound tax-payer-in-the-street. People like myself, who have been done down for too long by the sharks and charlatans[1] of the grab-now-pay-later variety! To put it at its simplest, Joe, I shall *not* be paying you with a fistful of readies but with a nice, clean cheque which you will then have to pay into your bank account.

JOE That's fine by me.

ALAN What?

JOE Yeah – a cheque's fine.

(*Pause*)

ALAN (*stunned*) Really?

JOE Why not? Makes no difference, does it?

HELEN (*in an undertone*) I think you owe someone an apology, darling.

ALAN Er . . . well . . .

JOE Only trouble is, of course . . .

ALAN Ah – here it comes! Wait for it! Wait for it!

JOE (*virtuously*) No, honest – I mean it's no skin off my nose – but you do realise that'll be fifteen per cent VAT on top?

ALAN *What?*

JOE I mean *I* don't mind – why should I? All goes to the government. I don't get any.

ALAN (*deeply affected*) Fifteen per cent . . .!

JOE Well of course I'd rather you had it than them – but if you feel that strongly . . .

ALAN Of course I wouldn't want to involve you in unnecessary paperwork . . . .

JOE Of course not. •

Tearing of paper.

1 frauds

HELEN   What are you tearing the cheque up for darling?

ALAN   (*the words stick in his throat*) If you could, er, if you could call round in a couple of days, Joe – when I've got the money out of the building society . . .

4 One month later

HELEN   (*admiringly*) Look at that! Now *that's* the sort of car you should be aiming for, darling. Smooth, elegant . . .

ALAN   Disgusting vulgar thing.

HELEN   You have got bitter recently, darling.

ALAN   What about our dwindling fuel supplies, eh?

HELEN   You don't think the job's getting on top of you?

ALAN   Look at him! He's stopping right next to our car – he's deliberately showing it up . . .

HELEN   Nonsense.

ALAN   (*wearily*) Oh no. I might have guessed – look who it is . . .

HELEN   (*delighted*) Joe! How nice . . .

ALAN   Kids at prep school . . . holidays in the Dordogne . . . new cars . . . who pays for it all?

HELEN   I don't know – who does?

ALAN   *Me*, that's who!

HELEN   Well not exactly darling – you still haven't paid him, after all. And it is over a month.

ALAN   Well he'll have to wait!

HELEN   But darling . . .

ALAN   I didn't slave my guts out for three years at university just for this.

HELEN   Just for what?

ALAN   I didn't sit up all night sweating over late Elizabethan poets on a paltry student's grant just to – just to line the pockets of some bloated working-class plutocrat.

HELEN   Joe's hardly bloated, darling. He's really rather slim.

ALAN   (*not listening*) I did it so we could have a good life together! You and me and the kids . . . So we could have a better life than people like him!!

HELEN   I still can't see what you're getting in such a state about, darling.

ALAN   I am not getting in such a state!!

HELEN   After all he has done the work. And made a very good
        job of it.

ALAN   Oh, I see ...

HELEN   (*bewildered*) What?

ALAN   So that's what you think, is it? I suppose wasting eight
        years of my life scrambling up from scale one to scale
        two to Head of Department to Deputy Head to
        Headmaster − I suppose *that* doesn't count as work?
        Pure bloody fun I suppose?

HELEN   Don't be silly darling.

        The doorbell rings.

        I'll go ...

ALAN   No you won't.

        He storms off.

HELEN   Do be careful darling ...

        Sound of front door being wrenched open.

JOE   Afternoon!

ALAN   (*maniacally bright*) Afternoon, Joe! You've come for your
        money, have you?

JOE   Well ...

ALAN   Well you can't have it, I'm afraid. I still haven't got it.

JOE   Ah.

ALAN   So what do you suggest we do?

JOE   Don't worry, don't worry ... That's why I come round.

ALAN   Really? You mean it wasn't to show off your new car?

JOE   No, that's the wife's. I'm getting my new one next week.

        Alan restrains himself with difficulty.

HELEN   Hello, Joe! How are you keeping?

JOE   Hello, Mrs ... er ... I was just saying to your old man −
        well I was just about to say ... I couldn't help noticing,
        the last few times I've been round −

HELEN   (*hastily*) We'll get your money very soon, don't worry.

JOE   No, no − that's it. I mean I noticed you were having a bit
        of trouble making ends meet ... and the wife was
        sorting out some old clothes the other day − well not all
        that old actually − but they don't fit the lad any
        more ... No offence, of course, but we wondered ...
        well we'd be very pleased if you'd accept them ...

A strangled cry from Alan.

HELEN   How very kind! Isn't it, darling?

Alan struggles to find words to express his feelings.

JOE   Come and have a look. They're in the car.

Sound of footsteps going to the car.

HELEN   It really is a lovely car.

ALAN   (*a weak distant voice*) I refuse . . .

HELEN   You know you must come round to dinner sometime. You and your wife.

JOE   Love to, yeah.

Car door being opened.

ALAN   (*feebly*) Darling please . . .!

Commence fade

HELEN   Such beautiful clothes . . .

Tick Tock
by *Jill Hyem*

The Cast

Grace *a charming, bed-ridden, old lady*
Louise *her long-suffering, middle-aged daughter*

As a clock ticks the night away, it reminds Louise of how her life is passing, looking after her invalid mother. At least she can look forward to a little holiday, until she reads the letter from her brother's wife. Suddenly, all the pent-up bitterness against her mother wells up, and threatens to turn the dutiful daughter into a murderer.

Tick Tock

A bedroom at night

Sound of a clock ticking, which continues throughout. Grace grunts as she struggles to shift her sleeping position. Sound of a cat yowling outside. Grace gasps. More cat sounds. Grace sighs as she recognises the sound.

GRACE Cats! (*More grunts of discomfort*) Oh it's no use. (*She feels for light switch*) Switch – switch – where is it? Ah.

She switches on bedside light. Then a grunt of exertion as she reaches out for the handbell on bedside table. As she rings it, she calls:

Louise!

As she rings bell again.

Louise!

We hear footsteps approaching off as Louise hurries downstairs.

LOUISE (*off*) I'm coming.

She opens door.

LOUISE (*from door*) What is it, Mother? (*Approaching anxiously*) Are you all right?

GRACE Yes, Yes. Did you think I'd had another stroke? I just can't get to sleep.

LOUISE (*with relief*) Oh.

GRACE And I can't reach my pills.

LOUISE You shouldn't have any more. You had two earlier.

GRACE Much good they did.

LOUISE No more than two, Dr Wainwright said.

GRACE *He* doesn't know what it's like to lie awake. Without even the luxury of being able to toss and turn.

LOUISE (*placatingly*) I'll have a word with him tomorrow, but best be on the safe side now – I'll make you a nice hot drink instead.

GRACE (*petulantly*) I don't want a hot drink.

LOUISE (*gently*) Let me tidy the bed clothes then. Make you comfier.

She does so.

GRACE (*penitently*) Sweet Louise ... Always so patient.

LOUISE Let's move you up a bit, shall we?

GRACE Did I wake you?

LOUISE No. I was – reading.

GRACE I wouldn't have rung only ... somehow at this hour everything seems so – bleak.

LOUISE I know ...

Louise moves her mother during the following. Sound of bedsprings etc.

GRACE (*deliberately*) Never mind. Five days and you'll be rid of me.

LOUISE That's no way to talk.

GRACE Gadding off with your school-chum, what's-a-name.

LOUISE Cynthia Bowers.

GRACE Such a stodgy girl. Staying with her's not my idea of fun.

LOUISE It's lovely country down there. It'll be a change.

GRACE No tiresome old mother to think about.

LOUISE Of course I'll think of you. Now roll onto your good side. That's it.

GRACE D'you realise it's the first time you've been away without me for – let's see –

LOUISE (*too quickly*) Ten years.

GRACE Since Daddy died.

LOUISE (*with a trace of intensity*) It's only for a week, Mother. Just a week.

GRACE When you're an invalid, a week can seem like eternity.

LOUISE You'll be with Philip and Janet.

GRACE I'll still miss my little girl.

LOUISE Hardly a little girl.

GRACE As far as I'm concerned you'll always be my little girl.

LOUISE I'm sure you'll have a marvellous time with them. Now for the pillows.

She puffs up pillows.

You're always saying you don't see enough of Philip.

GRACE I know how busy he is. But then he's a very important person these days. On the Board of Directors. Wouldn't Daddy have been proud?

LOUISE Wouldn't he?

GRACE And then he and Janet are always entertaining. Clients and so on. Such busy lives they lead. No time for me. But that's what you expect with a son, isn't it? "Your son's your son till he gains a wife –"

LOUISE *(dully)* "But your daughter's your daughter – all your life."

GRACE Truer word was never spoken.

LOUISE *(a little sharply)* Do you want to use the commode[1]?

GRACE No. If you could just move the hot water bottle round.

LOUISE Shall I fill you a fresh one?

GRACE No, I've been enough trouble already. A letter came for us, by the way. I'd forgotten.

LOUISE Letter? There you are.

Sound of a hot water bottle being moved.

GRACE From Philip and Janet. Mrs Hoskins met the postman on her way in yesterday. She put it on the shelf.

LOUISE *(attaching no importance to it)* It'll be the arrangements for Friday. Let's tuck these blankets in. They seem to've come adrift.

She tucks in the blankets.

GRACE Do you think Janet'll be collecting me in the new car?

LOUISE I daresay.

GRACE Fancy Philip with a Rolls. Remember how keen he was on cars as a boy? We used to give him those miniature ones.

LOUISE I remember.

GRACE The Rolls was his favourite even then. "You do well, and you'll have one of those when you grow up" Daddy used to say. *(Change of tone)* You don't think she'll come in the Mini, do you? I shouldn't be comfy in that.

---

1 chair with chamber pot under seat

LOUISE (*drily*) I expect she'll want to bring the Rolls.

GRACE If he lets her drive it.

LOUISE If not they'll send a hire car.

GRACE Oh I shouldn't like that.

LOUISE I wouldn't worry about it. If there are any problems we'll soon sort them out tomorrow.

GRACE Can't we read the letter now?

LOUISE (*wearily*) It's two o'clock, Mother.

GRACE I know I'm a nuisance ...

LOUISE It's waited since yesterday. A few more hours won't hurt.

GRACE (*winningly*) Please. To set Mummy's mind at rest.

LOUISE (*with forbearance, moving off*) All right.

GRACE (*after her*) It's on the shelf. There by the clock.

We go with Louise. Ticking of clock gets louder.

GRACE (*from bed*) What train are you catching on Friday?

LOUISE There's one after lunch.

She picks up letter.

Cynthia's going to meet me at Winchester. We want to potter round the bookshops, look at the Cathedral.

GRACE So Janet'll be fetching me first thing?

LOUISE (*moving to bed*) That's what I suggested.

She opens letter.

Shall I read it?

GRACE Please.

LOUISE (*reads*) "My dear Mother and Louise, we've tried to ring you several times without success."

GRACE That must've been when Mrs Hoskins left the phone off the hook.

LOUISE (*reads on, her voice gradually slowing up as she takes in what it says*) "The fact is something important has cropped up on the work front which will prevent us being able to have Mother here after all ..."

GRACE No!

LOUISE "I realise this will probably throw your plans a bit, but I'm afraid it's unavoidable."

Rustle of paper as she reads on.

(*Factually, slightly high-pitched, endeavouring to hide her emotion*) He goes on to explain that he and Janet have to go to this conference in Amsterdam. And to say that he hopes you'll be able to go there some other time.

(*Pause*)

GRACE (*only a little disappointed*) Oh well ... can't be helped. His work must come first. The penalty of having a successful son. And you'll be able to put your friend off in good time, won't you? Good thing you hadn't booked anywhere.

Louise screws paper up tightly.

(*Settling back with a little sigh*) You know in a way I'm quite relieved. I wasn't looking forward to all that upheaval. And Janet is such a hard girl. (*Cloyingly*) Not like my sweet Louise.

LOUISE (*in a strange voice*) "Sugar and spice and all things nice."

GRACE And so you are. I've been lucky with my daughter.

LOUISE (*with quiet intensity*) Luck? You call it luck?

GRACE What else?

LOUISE That wasn't luck, Mother.

GRACE What?

LOUISE *You* created me. You and father. Just as you made Philip what he is.

GRACE (*disconcerted by this change in Louise's manner*) I don't know what you mean.

LOUISE (*with a sharp laugh*) Born with a Silver Rolls, you might say. Public school, university trips abroad. He had the lot, didn't he?

GRACE We gave him every chance we could. Naturally. But –

LOUISE (*cuts in*) What was so *natural* about it?

GRACE Well –

LOUISE Go on. Tell me. I'd be interested to know.

GRACE He was our only son.

LOUISE Not your only child.

GRACE We couldn't afford private education for you both.

LOUISE *I* was the elder.

GRACE He was the boy.

LOUISE And that gave him some divine right?

GRACE What's the matter with you?

LOUISE (*continuing on*) He had *half* the intelligence I had.

GRACE He was a late-developer.

LOUISE You wouldn't have had to pay crammers to get me into a decent school.

GRACE He did well once he got there. He had the personality. The drive and ambition.

LOUISE You mean *you* had.

GRACE Louise!

LOUISE I can hear you now, goading him on. "Run faster, Philip, run faster. Win a prize for Mummy. Try harder, Philip, try harder, and Daddy'll buy you a bicycle."

GRACE A child needs incentives. We only . . .

LOUISE (*cuts in*) *I* didn't. But competitiveness in him was something to be encouraged. "Healthy aggression" you called it. While in me it was something to be subdued as unfeminine.

GRACE So it is. I hate aggressive females.

LOUISE You did a good job on me altogether, didn't you? Instilled all those admirable female virtues: gentleness, patience, sweetness.

GRACE There's nothing wrong with those.

LOUISE Taught me cookery, sewing, *acceptance*. Brainwashed me into thinking my one aim in life should be to find a suitable man. And having failed to do that, to fulfil that other female function – to stay at home and look after my parents.

GRACE We didn't force you to.

LOUISE You didn't need to. By then you had me trained.

GRACE That's not fair. You talk as though we held you back. You had your work at the library.

LOUISE Part-time librarian. Hardly stretching. Not for someone who wanted to be a barrister.

GRACE You never told us that.

LOUISE Oh yes I did. You don't even remember, do you? I was twelve at the time. There was still a small spark alight in me. You came in to say goodnight and I plucked up courage to tell you. Do you know what you did? You laughed.

GRACE Barrister's a man's job.

LOUISE That's what you said then.

GRACE And I still think so. I know some of these women's lib girls go into men's professions, but –

LOUISE They're not men's professions. They're anyone's profession. God, if only I was young now ...

Pause, clock ticking.

GRACE (*peevishly*) You always seemed to enjoy your work at the library.

LOUISE I enjoyed – getting out. But it was hardly a career was it? Not like Philip's job. Just a time-filler that could be conveniently dropped the minute I was needed here full-time.

GRACE I never realised how much you resented your brother.

LOUISE It's not him I resent. It's your attitude to him. Take now. He's let us down like this. Casually, without any thought of what it might mean to us ...

GRACE So that's it.

LOUISE ... and you calmly accept it, because it's *him*. Just as you automatically assume that "sweet Louise" will cancel her holiday. (*Her emotional and physical exhaustion apparent*) Never mind the fact that I needed that break as I've never needed anything before ...

(*Pause*)

GRACE Naughty Mummy. She didn't realise. Is my little girl very tired?

LOUISE (*with a bitter laugh*) Tired?

GRACE Of course she is.

LOUISE You don't know how tired!

GRACE Then of course she shall still go away. Mummy'll see to that. I'll ask Dr Wainwright to put me in one of those places.

LOUISE And you'll cry off like you did before. Crying off's a habit in this family.

GRACE It was you who said you couldn't leave me there.

LOUISE When you pleaded with me not to.

GRACE I'm sure I could survive it for a week, if it meant you having a rest.

LOUISE And I'd feel so guilty my holiday would become a penance. You're an expert on that, aren't you? Playing on my guilt. Why *should* I feel guilty? Philip isn't expected to.

GRACE This isn't my Louise talking.

LOUISE   Isn't it?

GRACE   No, no. But Mummy understands. You're at a difficult age.

LOUISE   I guessed that'd be coming.

GRACE   Mummy knows. Mummy went through it too.

LOUISE   When isn't a "difficult age" for women? People love sticking labels on us, don't they? People like Dr Wainwright. It's adolescence. It's sexual frustration. It's post partum[1] depression. It's the menopause. It's senile decay. As if sticking a label on changed anything. It just makes it easier to file you away.

GRACE   I don't know what's got into you tonight.

LOUISE   (*emotionally*) Nothing that wasn't there all the time. Buried, years back, along with all my hopes and ambitions.

GRACE   You've been drinking, I suppose.

LOUISE   Hah!

GRACE   I know you do sometimes. On the quiet, up in your room. I've smelt it on your breath.

LOUISE   What if I have! Is it surprising if I drink? (*with violence*) Christ, what else is there to do?

Grace dissolves into tears.

Oh no, not that.

A fractional halt in the crying.

Not the crocodile tears.

GRACE   (*through tears*) Why are you being so unkind?

LOUISE   Oh stop it, Mother.

GRACE   Anything I did in the past – I only did for the best.

LOUISE   Best for whom? For Philip. For yourself. Never for me.

Crying continues.

You've really got it to a fine art, haven't you? Even now you manage to cry prettily.

GRACE   Don't – please –

She continues to cry softly under the following.

LOUISE   That's something I could never do. But then I seldom cried. Except inside. Philip was the cry baby. But that

1 after giving birth

was cissy, wasn't it? Boys never cry. Only little girls, who learn to use tears as a weapon. Even when they're old.

GRACE I don't – it's not true.

LOUISE You do. I've seen you time and again. With Dr Wainwright, with Mrs Hoskins, with friends who look in. It's quite a performance. Dear old lady, dressed in lilac, grateful to everyone, never complaining, just weeping becomingly into a lace handkerchief. Would wring anyone's heart. Well my heart's empty. Hollow. Dead.

GRACE Please – please – I've got one of my headaches . . .

LOUISE *That* act now is it?

GRACE I have. I promise. I don't feel at all well.

LOUISE Nor do I! I feel sick to the stomach. When I think of what I've become. My life just ticking away like that bloody clock there.

Pause. The clock ticking peaks.

(*slowly*) And the most terrifying thing is that I could go on like this indefinitely. The hope of a week with Cynthia Bowers the only straw left to cling to. Imagine. Ten, fifteen years of this . . .

Peak ticking.

GRACE (*fearfully*) Don't look at me like that, Louise.

LOUISE (*sinister*) Like what, Mother?

GRACE I know what you're thinking.

LOUISE Do you?

GRACE If I was out of the way you'd be free.

LOUISE It's the only way I *can* be, isn't it?

GRACE You'll be rid of me soon. I could have another stroke any time.

LOUISE Dr Wainwright said it was unlikely. And even if you did, there's no guarantee it'd kill you.

Peak ticking.

No . . . there's only one answer, isn't there?

GRACE You don't know what you're saying.

LOUISE (*to herself*) The only way . . .

GRACE Don't be ridiculous, Louise.

LOUISE (*with a hysterical little laugh*) Sweet Louise, turned sour!

GRACE   Pull yourself together. You know you wouldn't hurt me. I'm your mother.

LOUISE   Wouldn't I?

Pause. Ticking and Louise breathing.

GRACE   (*a new ploy, wearily frail*) All right, then. Maybe you'd be doing me a favour too. You think I want to go on like this? Just a helpless invalid.

LOUISE   Oh you were never helpless. Even now – half paralysed – you're far from that.

GRACE   You could easily give me an overdose of those pills. Dr Wainwright would think I'd taken them myself.

LOUISE   Yes ... No one would ever suspect such a doting daughter. But pills are too risky.

GRACE   There are other ways.

LOUISE   Oh yes. Plenty. But they're either messy or unreliable. There's only one method I can think of that's foolproof.

GRACE   What's that?

LOUISE   I could suffocate you, couldn't I?
Snatching pillow up.
With this pillow!

A fearful moan from Grace.

Smother you, as you've smothered me, all my life!

We hear her breathing tensely as she stands poised over her mother.

GRACE   Go on then. What're you waiting for?

More breathing as Louise tries to steel herself to do it. But hesitates, unable to do it.

(*Seeing that she has won*) What are you waiting for, Louise? Kill me.

LOUISE   (*scarcely audible as she crumbles – defeated*) I – I – can't.

She lets go of pillow.

GRACE   Of course you can't.

LOUISE   (*letting out an almost animal cry of anguish*) Oh God! (*Then breaking down sobbing on bed – childlike*) Oh Mummy!

GRACE (*triumphant, comforting her as best she can*) There. There. It's all right. I've got you. I've got you. That's Mummy's girl.

Louise continues to sob. The clock continues to tick, drowning her crying.

Taurus
by Sam Smith

CAPRICORN AQUARIUS PISCES ARIES TAURUS GEMINI LEO VIRGO LIBRA SCORPIO SAGITTARIUS

VIRGO
August 24 to September 23

TAURUS
APR 21–MAY 20

CHESS/Leonard Barden

Garfield by Jim Davis

The Cast

Mike *eager young journalist, born under Virgo*
Sandra *astrology-conscious girl of his dreams; Taurus*
Malcolm *Mike's go-ahead young editor*

*Mike is cunning, confident and resourceful in every way –
except one. Not taking astrology seriously, he thinks he can
manipulate Sandra's fate by writing her horoscope. He can,
but not as he intends, for he cannot escape his own fate.*

Taurus

1 The meeting

MIKE Well, I'll tell you, the flat downstairs had been empty for a few weeks, then one day, when I was at work, *she* moved in. It's my second job I'm on now, the first was labouring on a building site. Well, I said to myself, 'Mike Taylor, you're in a dead end job', so ... I got a job with the local paper, nothing special – just filing. Same as labouring really, only instead of stacking bricks I was piling files up. Boring. Mind you, it did have some advantages. I got this 'press card'. I put it in the car window – nothing flash mind – just left it like I'd dropped it and forgotten to pick it up. Thought it might help, with girls, you know ... It didn't though. Total failure. Anyway, as I said, *she* moved in downstairs ...

Sandra her name was, and attractive. The sort of girl who when she walks down the street causes a lot of married men to get a dig in the ribs from the wife. Anyway, it wasn't so much the way she looked, but the way she spoke, whew! So the next day I was a bit extravagant, bought a couple of steaks, bottle of wine ... you know, the 'I'm your neighbour' touch – well, you've got to try, haven't you? So, nipped downstairs, knocked on the door, and she spoke ...

SANDRA Yes?

MIKE Well, that was that, one word ... one word, so I asked her and she said she'd come up. Then we had the meal, opened the wine and started chatting.

Small room. Wine glasses being filled.

MIKE ... Of course, I'm not doing anything important, not yet, but who knows, once I've learnt the trade New York ... Fleet Street ...

SANDRA   Does your paper have a horoscope?

MIKE   Horoscope? No ... Why?

SANDRA   That's all I buy papers for.

MIKE   Horoscopes? You're joking! You don't believe all that do you?

Horoscope, that was it, the "entry". A bit vague at first but that night I came up with the idea, so first thing in the morning I was in the editor's office. Young bloke he was, not bad, gave us all a fair crack of the whip. Malcolm his name was, Malcolm Trott, and he fell for the horoscope idea hook, line and sinker – mind you, I'd done my homework ...

2 Editor's office

Distant sounds of typing and telephones.

MALCOLM   ... but will it sell papers Mike?

MIKE   (*in a 'I-really-want-to-sell-you-this' voice*) Well Malcolm, I think it will. Now, the results aren't conclusive, but I've done a fair bit of research ...
(*Aside*) It was a lie but it sounded impressive.
... Nothing special, just in pubs and on the bus, and did you know, that out of five hundred people, four hundred and ninety of them read the horoscope! Just look at these figures ...

Rustle of paper.

(*Aside*) What I always say is, that if you're going to con someone, set it up right – I'd made those figures up over breakfast.
Now Malcolm, here look, out of the two hundred and eighty who don't buy our paper, one hundred and ninety five said that its not having a horoscope was one of the reasons, and that, Malcolm ...
(*Aside*) Thank God for pocket calculators ...
... is sixty nine point six per cent! You reach just half that figure on an overall sales basis, and that, Malcolm, *that* is selling newspapers!

MALCOLM   OK, Mike. I'm a man of instant decisions, I'll give it a try. So, where can I get an astrologist?

MIKE   Look no further! You see Malcolm, I've been doing all this for two reasons ...

(*Aside*) Both of them Sandra's – but I wasn't going to tell Malcolm that ...

You see Malcolm I'm really into astrology, have been for years. I can do it, Malcolm.

MALCOLM Mike, you've got the job.

MIKE Thanks Malcolm. That brings me to the second reason ... You see, if this paper's going to grow, I want to grow with it. This could be really great, for us both.

(*Aside*) This boy should be selling encyclopaedias ...

MIKE So that was that, enter Xenon Kallendo – me that is, Mike Taylor. Well ... the next Wednesday night, when the paper came out, I casually called in to see Sandra on my way upstairs ...

3 Sandra's flat

Knock and door opens.

SANDRA Hello Mike.

MIKE (*aside*) See what I mean about the voice?
(*miserably*) Hello Sandra.

SANDRA You sound a bit down in the dumps. Want some coffee?

MIKE Thanks.

Door shuts.

No, I'm a bit choked really. See, I'd got this date, table booked for dinner, then right at the last minute she cried off. Stood me up.

Rattle of cups.

SANDRA That's a shame, never mind, here's the coffee.

MIKE Ta. By the way, did I tell you we've got a horoscope in the paper now?

SANDRA Really?

MIKE Yeah, not a bad bloke so it seems, gipsy, got quite a reputation.

SANDRA Have you got it with you?

MIKE Hmm. Shall I read it out?

SANDRA Please. Sugar?

Rustle of newspaper.

MIKE Two ta. What's your sign then?

(*Aside*) As if I didn't know!

SANDRA   Taurus.

MIKE   The bull huh? Right, let's see, Taurus, "A routine week, life plods on at its usual pace. A chance remark could lead to an unexpected treat, but it's up to you to take the bull by the horns." Load of old cobblers!

SANDRA   No it's not, that was good. It has been a routine week.

MIKE   Every week's routine.

SANDRA   No they're not, some weeks are very hectic.

MIKE   What's this other bit then, "A chance remark could lead to an unexpected treat ... up to you to take the bull by the borns?"

SANDRA   Well ... it means somebody's going to make a chance remark and ... Ah! I know what it means. You remember you said you'd been stood up?

MIKE   Yes.

SANDRA   Well, that's a chance remark, and if you take *me* out to dinner instead, that's the unexpected treat, and my suggesting it is taking the bull by the horns. So there, true.

MIKE   So that was it, master stroke, and that was just the start. Every week the paper printed the horoscope, and every week Taurus was spot on. One week she bought some new curtains, so her stars said: "Something you've bought this week makes your home more attractive – now is the time to celebrate." And another week she pulled off some sort of master stroke at work, so Taurus said: "Favourable career developments have concentrated your efforts at work, but don't forget those at home ...". Good one that – just to celebrate she paid for the meal. But we weren't really getting anywhere – know what I mean – well, she held my hand once, but seeing as how we were on the back row of the pictures, I reckon she could've done better, so the next week, I thought I'd give her a nudge in the right direction ...

4 Sandra's room

SANDRA   Taurus, "Life is full and pleasant at the moment but time waits for no man. If you haven't put down roots yet, now is the time to start." It's true, you know.

MIKE   Rubbish.

SANDRA   No it is. I've been thinking. You see ... work's all right, but I sometimes think I'm missing out on something ...

MIKE   How do you mean?

SANDRA   Well ... I don't know really. All my friends are married. I just think I'm missing out. I think I should put down roots.

MIKE   Hey, you don't want to talk about things like that. Getting married! No, you enjoy yourself while you can.

SANDRA   I don't know. Don't you ever feel, well, a little bit like that ...

MIKE   (*aside*) Take it steady Michael old son, don't rush into this one.

SANDRA   (*musing*) I suppose if I did put down roots, if I had to choose, he'd have to believe in horoscopes.

MIKE   Horoscopes! Not that again.

SANDRA   Why not! Just look at all the times it's been right.

MIKE   Coincidence. Mind you, I've got to grant it, we're none of us getting any younger ...

And so it went on. Quite a successful evening really, she got the idea, and I got a goodnight kiss. Nothing heavy mind, just a peck, but progress all the same.

Well, with that, it's up into second gear and pile on the pressure. Things like:

"Someone near you is getting closer" and "Be especially nice to someone you're fond of". Whew, what! If they ever start psychological warfare they ought to make me a general. General Michael ... No, hang about, General Sir Michael Taylor. Got a bit of a ring to it.

So, I said to myself, now is the time to increase the pressure – both mental and physical if you get my drift. Very pneumatic[1] girl is Sandra ... So next week: "Someone you're very fond of has become very special. Make an extra effort now lest the chance slip through your fingers." That should do the trick, I thought, so instead of calling in on the way home, I

1 impressionable (mentally) and well-padded (physically)

went straight upstairs, you know, the "slipping through the fingers" act. A quick tidy round, swop the light bulb for a cosy red one, bit of soft music, and wait for it ...

Fade out.

5 Mike's room

Sentimental music in background. Knock on door and door opens.

SANDRA (*hesitant*) Hello Mike.
MIKE Oh. (*Aside*) Act surprised.
Hello Sandra ...
SANDRA I'm sorry, have I ... come at the wrong time?
MIKE No, no. I was just getting ready to go out that's all.
SANDRA Anything special?
MIKE No ... well ... no ...

Cor, talk about below the belt! Well, she'd brought a couple of bottles of plonk with her, so ... I let her persuade me to stay in. Funny about that 'slipping through the fingers' bit though, she didn't let go of me all night. Can't be bad, can it? You know, I reckon there must be a lot of people going out with a Taurus who've got a lot to thank me for.
Well, it was nice while it lasted but I reckon all good things should have the chance of getting better, so it was a nice vague ... "You have reached a point in your life when you must make a decision." There was only one way Sandra would take that. And she did. That was the night she cornered me ...

SANDRA Mike, I've got to make a decision ...
MIKE Pardon.
SANDRA I've got to make a decision. It was in the stars.
MIKE Not that again.
SANDRA I'm serious Mike. I've a decision to make, and if it was a choice ... I'd ... If I had to choose between two ... well ... I'd choose the one who shared my belief in fate.
MIKE (*aside*) Steady son, she could go the wrong way on this one.
Astrology?

SANDRA	Yes.
MIKE	(*aside*) Play it carefully ...
	Do you think you ... (*blurts out*) do you think you could teach me about it?
SANDRA	(*as if leaping into his arms*) Oh yes Mike, yes!
MIKE	Phew, close call that. Didn't like the "choose between two" bit. Expertly handled though. In fact, things were going well all round ...

6 Malcolm's office

Typing and telephones.

MALCOLM	Well Mike, what do you make of this?
MIKE	It's a graph, Malcolm.
MALCOLM	And which way is it going, Mike? I'll tell you. It's going up! Sales figures, Mike. Sales figures. And look at the date it started. 24th April. Mean anything?
MIKE	Not off hand, Malcolm.
MALCOLM	The first day of your horoscope feature, Mike!
MIKE	Well I'm blowed.
MALCOLM	It's going well Mike. Very well. And to show my thanks ... a small increase in salary and ... wait! Promotion. I want you to handle the births, marriages and deaths column!
MIKE	So, promotion – and it didn't stop there, it wasn't long before I was covering all the crime stories in the local courts! Mike Taylor, crime reporter. And I didn't forget Sandra, oh no, listen to this ... "Make a special effort this week, someone in Virgo needs your special attention." And with that little gem I was rubbing me hands waiting for Sandra to come up for my regular astrology lesson.

7 Mike's room

SANDRA	Do you enjoy our lessons Mike?
MIKE	(*aside*) Keep cool Michael. (*Aloud*) Pardon?
SANDRA	I was just wondering if you enjoyed our lessons together.
MIKE	(*aside*) Gently does it son ... (*Aloud*) Yes ... I think I do.
SANDRA	Are you a Virgo Mike?
MIKE	Virgo! Me? Oh, ah September yes.
SANDRA	(*she sobs*) Oh Mike. (*Changing to anger*) You don't

believe, do you! You don't even know your own birth sign!

Slamming of door.

MIKE Well, as you may gather, this was serious. I wanted her to move in not out! So the next week I decided to put things right. Taurus got it with both barrels. "Today is the most important day of your life, it is a day for final decisions. Lucky initials M. T." M. T. Get it? M. T. Mike Taylor – me. A bit strong perhaps but things were a bit desperate, no time to hang about, so you can imagine the shock when I got home and saw the "To Let" notice in Sandra's window. The landlady said she'd come in just after lunch with the paper under her arm, paid what was due, packed her bags and left. Bit of a poser that, but there was only one thing to do.

"Taurus. It's not too late to change your mind if any action you've taken now seems rash." Not a word though, not a dickybird. Well, it rocked me a bit because I started hitting the old bottle, then a few weeks later I was just going to the pub after work . . . and walked straight into her! Thing I noticed straight off was the wedding ring. With a little surprise like that, you can imagine how much attention I was paying. Can't remember what she said but one thing sticks in the mind, as she was leaving: In that voice.

SANDRA I could never marry a man who didn't really believe in the stars. I'm sorry Mike, but I found a man who really does.

MIKE And so she went, just like that. So I went straight into the pub, and just about to line up the old bottles, when blow me, the door bursts open and who should come waltzing in but . . .

Public bar.

(*Surprised*) Malcolm!

MALCOLM (*full of himself*) Mike! Hello! Hello, hello, hello. Let me get you a drink. What's that you've got? Whisky? Good. Barman! Two doubles please.

MIKE (*not full of himself*) You seem very pleased with yourself.

MALCOLM And so I am, so I am. I'm going to be a father! *Me* a father!

MIKE I didn't even know you were courting.

MALCOLM It was so quick Mike, so quick – I'm not sure I believe it myself sometimes. Right out of the blue. (*Lapses into opening time G-and-T-set monologue[1]*)

It was in a pub, one lunchtime, few colleagues, ad hoc conference, you know the sort of thing, and one of the chaps had this girl with him. Well you know me Mike, man of instant decisions, and – I – decided she was *a* girl. So we started chatting, she told me what she did, I told her about me, you know, editor of one of the larger provincials ... Anyway I knew I was well-known round here but when I told her my name was Malcolm Trott, talk about doe-eyed attention! And – this will interest you Mike – you know what the next thing she says was? Horoscopes. Do you believe in horoscopes?

MIKE (*gulp*) Horoscopes, Malcolm?

MALCOLM Horoscopes, Mike, and do you know, funny thing, but this happened the very day you and I had gone through the new sales figures. Well, with figures we'd come up with what else could I do? So I said, "Horoscopes," I said, "I believe passionately in horoscopes."

MIKE Passionately?

MALCOLM Quite. And do you know, before I could say another word it was arms round my neck and Bob's your uncle[2]. Well it seems her stars said something about the initials M. T. being lucky, so she proposed. And there you have it. Married. Anyway, must dash.

Puts glass on bar.

See you Monday, Mike. (*Receding*) Can't keep Sandra waiting.

Sound of pub swing door.

---

1 the sort of solo speech you give to a group drinking gin and tonic
2 everything's settled. A. J. Balfour rose swiftly in government when his uncle Robert, Lord Salisbury, was Prime Minister.

MIKE *(strangled)* Oh no. Sandra. M. T. She's only gone and married Malcolm bloody Troot.

Sound of pub swing door.

MALCOLM Oh, by the way, Mike, just to show you how quick it was, do you know, I've still not told her about the circulation figures.

And No Birds Sing

by *Ted Willis*

The Cast

Ann *Philip's all-too-normal wife*
Philip *a poetry-loving businessman*
Syms *a painstaking detective sergeant*

*Philip has caught the same early train home two days run-
ning, and is accused of assaulting two schoolgirls. His wife's
reaction, and his own ambiguous attitude, make us wonder
what really happened while he was reading Keats's famous
romantic poem.*

And No Birds Sing

Philip and Ann's house

Sound of doorbell chiming

ANN   (*calls*) Door. (*Moves nearer*) Philip – *door*!

PHIL   (*tetchy*) Oh, for God's sake! I'm trying to read.

ANN   I'm trying to get the dinner. I can't do everything. See who it is and get rid of them.

PHIL   I came home early to get a little peace!

Sound of doorbell chiming.

(*moving*) All right, all right – I'm coming, I'm coming!

Sound of Phil's footsteps, and click of door opening.

Yes?

SYMS   Mr Brooks?

PHIL   Yes, What is it?

SYMS   I wonder if I might have a word –

PHIL   What about?

SYMS   Perhaps – if we could talk inside?

PHIL   (*puzzled*) Why? What's – are you from the police?

SYMS   That's an odd question, sir. You've been expecting the police to call, have you?

PHIL   No – no. Of course not –

SYMS   (*heavy humour*) Nothing on your conscience, eh? Yes, all right, Mr Brooks. I'm from Woodgate CID. Detective Sergeant Syms. I'm making certain enquiries in connection with –

PHIL   Look. Perhaps you'd better come in.

SYMS   Thank you, sir.

Sounds of door closing.

ANN   (*distant*) Who was it? Philip –

PHIL   (*calls*) Just a sec. (*To·Syms*) My wife.

Sound of another door opening.

If you'd wait here – in the lounge – won't be a moment.

2 The kitchen

Sound of dripping tap.

ANN I wish you'd fix this tap, Philip. It's driving me mad. Drip – drip – drip. Who was that?

PHIL A policeman.

ANN A what?

PHIL Let me do that. (*Grunts as he tightens tap*) A policeman. There. You just need to tighten the tap, that's all.

ANN I'm not Tarzan. What it needs is a new washer. You've been going to do it for weeks. What did he want?

PHIL I don't know.

ANN What do you mean?

PHIL He's still here. In the lounge.

ANN The dinner's almost ready! Oh, Philip –

PHIL I can't help it. You carry on – I'll get rid of him as soon as I can.

ANN You haven't been speeding or anything?

PHIL No, no. It's a CID man. They wouldn't send CID for that.

ANN (*curious*) CID! Mm-mm There – the dinner should be all right for a few minutes. I'll come in with you.

PHIL No. There's no point in you getting involved.

ANN Involved? What do you mean –

PHIL Look, don't take me up on every word –

ANN It's a curious word to use. Involved. You've no idea what –

PHIL (*each word deliberate*) I – have – no – idea – at – all. All right – if you're coming, come.

Sound of dripping tap fades.

3 The lounge

SYMS You travel to town by train every day, Mr Brooks?

PHIL (*terse*) Every day – except Saturdays and Sundays.

SYMS And return home by train?

PHIL I don't *walk* home. Yes – I come home by train.

SYMS Did you catch your normal train home today?

PHIL (*slight hesitation*) No.

SYMS Oh?

PHIL I decided – it was so damned hot in London – I decided to come home early, bring some work with me. I knocked off early and caught the 3.50 to Woodgate.

SYMS You also caught the same train yesterday afternoon?

PHIL Yes.

SYMS Do you own a briefcase? A black, slimline briefcase bearing the initials PJB?

PHIL (*savage*) Hardly surprising – since they are my initials!

SYMS Do you also own a – (*Pause*) – a volume of poetry called – (*Pause*) – "Other Men's Flowers"[1]?

PHIL Is that what I'm accused of – a liking for poetry?

SYMS Mr Brooks, you are not being accused of anything – yet. I'm only trying to establish . . .

PHIL What? What? You come here, you ask a lot of stupid questions . . .

ANN Philip – please, you're not making it any easier.

PHIL (*mocking*) Oh. I am so sorry. I do apologise, Sergeant. Only you have me at a disadvantage, don't you see? You know what this is about, and I haven't a blasted clue!

SYMS (*impassive*) Are you sure of that, Mr Brooks?

PHIL Good God, man, I've been waiting for the – (*Checks – a note of pleading*) What is it?

SYMS (*reading from notebook, his voice flat, formal and fast*) At 6 p.m. this evening I received a complaint from the mothers of two young girls. They allege that their daughters were improperly assaulted . . .

ANN Oh, no!

SYMS . . . on their way home from school. They further allege that the incident took place in a railway carriage on the 3.50 train from Croydon to Woodgate.

ANN You are surely not suggesting –

SYMS The briefcase carried by this man was inscribed with the initials PJB. The girls further allege that the offence was committed by a middle-aged man wearing a dark grey suit who had travelled on the same train with them – in the same carriage – the previous afternoon . . .

ANN Philip –

---

[1] the best-known English poems, printed to boost soldiers' morale during the war

SYMS   . . . they also allege that when they entered the carriage at Redfurn the man was reading a volume of poetry – an anthology called "Other Men's Flowers", a collection made by the late Field-Marshal Wavell.

ANN   This is ridiculous. My husband would –

SYMS   Their statement goes on to say that the man in question left the train at Woodgate Station. The Head Porter remembered seeing him at the barrier and confirmed that he was a season ticket holder. We checked the register of people with season tickets and found only one person with the initials PJB. A Mr Philip James Brooks of this address.

PHIL   (a whisper) What am I supposed – supposed to have done?

SYMS   The charge – the charge would be one of indecent assault. Do you wish to make a statement, sir?

ANN   No! No, he does not! Philip – don't say a word! Sergeant – we wish to contact out solicitor.

SYMS   That is your privilege, madam. I have further enquiries to pursue. But I shall have to ask you to come to Woodgate Station in the morning for the purpose of making a formal statement. And it may be necessary to ask you to take part in an identification parade. Shall we say 9.30 a.m., sir?

PHIL   It isn't true, you know that. None of it is true. It's all lies.

SYMS   We are careful in all such cases, sir. That is why I am pursuing my enquiries. Thank you, sir. 9.30 a.m. – Woodgate Station.

PHIL   They've made it up. Those girls – it's lies – all lies – lies – they're lying!

SYMS   Goodnight, sir. Madam.

Sound of footsteps.

4 Later that evening

John Neville recording of "La Belle Dame Sans Merci".

RECORD   'O what can ail thee, knight-at-arms,
So haggard and so woe-begone?
The squirrel's granary is full
And the harvest's done.'

ANN   (distant) Philip –

RECORD 'I see a lily on thy brow
With anguish moist and fever-dew,
And on thy cheeks a fading rose ...

Door opens, recording is clicked off.

ANN Philip! How can you sit here listening to that stuff at a time like this!?

PHIL That *stuff* is poetry.

ANN You've been up here, shut away, for the last hour. Have you forgotten what happened this evening?

PHIL "Better by far you should forget and smile Than that you should remember and be sad."[1]

ANN I've tried Barker – the solicitor – a dozen times. There's no reply.

PHIL It doesn't matter.

ANN Of course it matters! This – this terrible thing. You need help, Philip. God – if this gets out, if a whisper of it gets out. (*Pause*) Philip – what happened on that train? What did happen?

PHIL Don't you know?

ANN How can I know!

PHIL Don't you know me?

ANN (*defensively*) Of course. I mean – well – naturally – this accusation – I mean – I know it can't be true.

PHIL (*with a touch of irony*) Thank you, dear.

ANN And I intend to stand by you. I'm your wife, after all.

PHIL Let's never forget that.

ANN But if I'm to help, I must know.

PHIL Know what?

ANN What happened. Exactly what happened.

PHIL I told you – nothing. Nothing.

ANN Something must have happened. Those girls – they gave your description. And there was the book of poems ...

PHIL Oh, it was me all right.

ANN What!

PHIL It was me – on the train. I saw the two girls, they were in my carriage.

ANN And?

PHIL That's all.

1 from "Remember" by Georgina Rossetti

Pause, and then sound of window shutting.

Don't close the window!

ANN   The light. We don't want the room full of moths.

PHIL Moths never harmed anyone.

ANN   I hate them. (*Pause*) Philip – you told that policeman that you had brought some work home from the office – you told him that was why you left early.

PHIL Well?

ANN   You didn't. I checked your case. You brought some papers home yesterday. Not today.

PHIL So. I got the days mixed up.

ANN   It is important that you tell the truth – the absolute exact truth.

PHIL Oh, my God.

Sound of match striking.

ANN   Philip – please – I've asked you a hundred times not to smoke your pipe in the – (*Checks*) All right. It doesn't matter – if you need to smoke – (*Pause*) Philip – you came home early twice – two days running. Why?

PHIL Because I'd had London – the office – had it up to here.

ANN   And on both days you travelled in the same carriage with those girls? Don't you think that was rather foolish?

PHIL I didn't think so at the time – but I do now.

ANN   The first day – yesterday – I can understand. But two days running. How old were they?

PHIL Children. Thirteen–fourteen. Hard to tell nowadays.

ANN   What were they wearing?

PHIL Wearing?

ANN   Were they in school uniform? Gym tunics – that sort of thing?

PHIL No. Dresses. They were wearing dresses.

ANN   You noticed that. Philip – *did* you – did you touch them?

PHIL Yes. As the train went through Burford tunnel I raped them, one after the other.

ANN   Philip – if I'm to help you –

PHIL I don't want your bloody help! I just want you to believe me. To believe *in* me.

ANN   I'm only trying to –

PHIL Trying to what?

ANN To get the tru ... the facts, the real facts.

PHIL The real facts, as you so tactfully put it, are very simple. Yesterday, the two girls got into my carriage. They seemed nice kids, fresh, cheeky, but nice enough. They saw that I was reading a book of poetry and began to giggle. Must have thought it odd.

ANN It *is* odd.

PHIL So we talked a bit.

ANN About what?

PHIL Poetry.

ANN Nothing else?

PHIL Yes. I gave them a lecture on sex.

ANN Philip, this isn't a joking matter!

PHIL It was a simple, casual, ordinary meeting.

ANN That was yesterday. What about today?

PHIL The same.

ANN You discussed poetry.

PHIL And smoking.

ANN Smoking?

PHIL One of them – the dark-haired one –

ANN Dark-haired?

PHIL Well, sort of chestnut-coloured really. The other was blonde.

ANN (*grim*) I see.

PHIL The dark-haired one took out some cigarettes, and offered me one. I said I only smoked a pipe. Then she asked me for a light.

ANN And you obliged!

PHIL I asked them what their parents would say about them smoking but they just laughed. So –

ANN So you gave her a light.

PHIL Yes.

ANN How?

PHIL How? For God's sake, how do you give anyone a light? (*Deliberate*) I took a box of matches from my pocket, I withdrew a match, I struck it with an upwards movement of the hand and then I held it out, towards the girl's cigarette.

ANN The train was moving at the time.

PHIL Of course the blasted train was moving!

ANN It's difficult, holding a lighted match in a moving train.

All that swaying about. How did you manage?

PHIL   Ann – stop it, stop it!

ANN   Did you hold her wrist – to keep the cigarette steady?

PHIL   I don't know! I suppose I might have done.

ANN   Then you *did* touch her!

PHIL   Ann, for God's sake!

ANN   Did that make you want to touch her again? You were close to her, you must have been. Did you want to touch her again?

PHIL   Ann – go away – take a couple of pills – knock yourself out!

ANN   That's what you went back for, isn't it? You caught the early train today because you wanted to see those girls. Especially the one with chestnut hair ... you went back to see her, to touch her.

PHIL   (*a pause*) I thought I might *see* them both. Yes. *See* them.

ANN   (*a huge sigh*) Ah. At last.

PHIL   Not what you think. It wasn't even a conscious thought on my part. I really did want to get out of London. And when they got into the carriage I was glad to see them. They – they were – so fresh, eager, full of life.

ANN   They were children! Schoolgirls! Children!

PHIL   I know.

ANN   Disgusting!

PHIL   No. It wasn't disgusting. Stupid, maybe. Stupid. I don't expect you to believe me – but I never saw or thought of them as other than children. Do you know – sitting with them there – I felt – I felt almost sad. You know? Sad. I'm fifty one years old, and I felt the weight of each single year. The dark-haired girl had an ink-stain on her thumb. I saw it when I lit the cigarette. I used to get ink all over my hands at school ...

ANN   I don't want to hear!

PHIL   No. You never do really, do you? You listen, but you don't hear. You haven't heard me for a long time.

Sound of a telephone, distant.

ANN   The phone.

PHIL   Yes.

ANN   Well, aren't you going to answer it?

PHIL   I don't think so.

ANN   You're impossible!

The door slams. Pause, phone stops. Then click of recording.

RECORD 'I met a lady in the meads,
Full beautiful – a faery's child,
Her hair was long, her foot was light
And her eyes were wild.

I made a garland for her head,
And bracelets too, and fragrant zone.
She looked at me as she did love,
And made sweet moan.'

Sound of door opening and closing.

ANN Philip. Philip!

PHIL I'm trying to listen . . .

Click as recorder goes off.

ANN That was the police! It's all right. Philip. It's all right! One of the girls broke down, told them that they'd made it all up as a joke!

PHIL A joke. (*Laughs*) A joke! Very humorous.

ANN I told the police I wasn't satisfied! I mean – such lies! I said we would take it further. To accuse you! Philip – you will do something? See the parents, at least –

PHIL I'll see. In the morning.

ANN Come down. The dinner's still eatable.

PHIL In a moment. You go.

ANN Philip . . .

PHIL Yes?

ANN I never really doubted – you know.

PHIL I know.

The door opens and closes. Click of recording.

RECORD "And I awoke and found me here
On the cold hill's side.

And this is why I sojourn here
Alone and palely loitering,
Though the sedge is withered from the lake,
And no birds sing."

Microcosm
by *J. C. Wilsher*

The Cast

Old Man *a retired engineer with a Sheffield accent*
Visitor *a youth with an interest in model-making*

The old man has never shown anyone his model collection before – the visitor is the first person to express any interest. Fascinated by the skill, the craftsmanship and the historical details, it is some time before the visitor realises that these are no mere replicas. There is something mysteriously sinister going on in the old man's miniature world.

The visitor could easily be female, with a few slight changes.

Microcosm

The old man's place

Sound of a door being unlocked.

OLD MAN As long as yer really interested, lad ... I don't like ter think you'd be bored sick, lookin' at my old junk ...

VISITOR I keep telling you, I really want to see it. Why else do you think I've been feeding you draught Guinness every lunchtime since you told me ...

OLD MAN (*chuckles*) Well, it wouldn't appeal ter most folk, I don't suppose – still, yer an educated feller, 'appen that makes a difference. Down here – mind these steps, now – I'll put light on ...

They are descending into a large domestic cellar.

VISITOR Oh ... This is really something! I expected – I don't know, perhaps a model railway layout; or a couple of ships in bottles; or a working model of a steam engine ... But all these display cases – it's like the Science Museum!

OLD MAN Aye, well, it's built up to quite a collection, over the years ... I've 'ad a go at the sort of things yer talkin' about, model railways, a boat that used ter chug across pond wi' a little petrol engine, an' I made a model Boulton and Watt beam engine once – on forty-eighth scale, wi' separate condenser an' sun and planet gear[1], all authentic ... But it's these little displays I've allus 'ad me 'eart in, since I were fust apprenticed ... Not just followin' scaled-down plans, but mekkin' a little bit o' world in miniature, capturin' a moment o' time ... More room fer imagination, I suppose ... (*Pause*) Well, where shall we start ...?

---

1 early type of gear, in which the smaller wheel drives the bigger by rotating round it

VISITOR	Why don't you show them to me in the order that you made them? What's the oldest?
OLD MAN	Over 'ere ... I did this one when I were fust apprenticed, back in 1912 ...
VISITOR	An ocean liner. Must've been a big one, all the little cabins and portholes ...
OLD MAN	Three thousand, six 'undred and nine aboard, on fifteenth of April 1912 ... (*Pause*) It's the *Titanic*, lad ...
VISITOR	Yes, of course! And there's the iceberg in the background ...
OLD MAN	Aye, well, I 'ad ter cheat a bit wi' that, yer can't get much in the way o' technical specifications fer icebergs ... I think it come out all right, though ...
VISITOR	It's marvellous! Superb detail – all the little lifeboats ...
OLD MAN	Lucky there weren't any more, they took ages ter get right ...
VISITOR	... And you were, what, fourteen when you did this?
OLD MAN	Aye ... 'Course, I'd not the *skill* in them days, but 'appen I made up wi' nimbler fingers an' sharper eyes ...
VISITOR	Fourteen – you'd have been just the generation for the First War, then ...?
OLD MAN	Aye, but I were well on the way ter bein' a craftsman by then. I were put on munitions instead o' bein' called up ... That's what put me on to this next 'un, 'ere ...
VISITOR	A factory, with the roof cut away ... Yes, a munitions factory, of course. Women working on shells at the benches – I suppose those notices on the walls are safety regulations ...?
OLD MAN	Aye ... Didn't stop it goin' up though – 1916. Biggest bang ever 'eard in London. Silvertown munitions factory.
VISITOR	And this model's contemporary with the event, again – I mean you did it in 1916?
OLD MAN	(*as if this is obvious*) Oh aye, well, that's the whole point ...
VISITOR	(*thinking he understands*) ... Recording the historical moment for posterity, yes, of course. Did you actually make models of events in the actual *fighting*? I realise

your interest is in technology, but I mean, oh, aircraft being used for warfare for the first time, or the tanks breaking through at Cambrai ...

OLD MAN (*very slightly irritated as if the point has been missed*) No, lad, that's not what I were after ... 'Ave a look at a couple more, these 'ere ...

VISITOR Airships ... This smaller one's got part of the skin cut away, so you can see, well, bags of gas. I suppose they are ...

OLD MAN There were seventeen altogether ... filled wi' hydrogen. Y'know what they were made of? (*Pause*) ... Bullocks' intestines! Don't seem credible now ... if y'look close y'can see inside gondola, where passengers were ...

VISITOR That's splendid – but they really had *potted palms* in this thing?

OLD MAN Aye, an' six 'undred feet of 'eavy Axminster carpet ... It were grossly overloaded, on maiden flight to India – I've shown it passin' over countryside near Beauvais, that's northern France.

VISITOR Yes, the ... er ... scenery and background look really good ...

OLD MAN That's what we call the *diorama*. It failed to clear one o' these low 'ills, an' bust into flames ... Fifty-four on board an' forty-seven killed. The R101.

VISITOR ... So *this* one must be the *Hindenburg*; I've seen the film of that going up in flames. It had just crossed the Atlantic, right?

OLD MAN (*pleased that his guest is getting it right*)
That's it, just arrived at Lakenhurst, New Jersey from Frankfurt ... I've got it just about to tie up at its mast, there – sixth o' May, 1937. Ninety-seven on board, thirty-six killed ... By 'eck, all this talkin's parched me throat. Would y'care fer a cup o' tea?

VISITOR Oh ... But there's so much more to see down here ...

OLD MAN Oh, we're not goin' upstairs yet, lad, I've got all the makin's down 'ere, 'andy fer me work bench ... sink, 'lectric kettle ...

Sound of running water into kettle.

I rarely stir from down 'ere these days, 'cept fer shops,

an' pub at lunchtime, o'course ... I've got me wireless 'ere, ter keep up wi what's on in't world. Our lass[1] used ter watch telly of an evenin' when she were with us, but I could never be bothered wi' it meself, carried on down 'ere at me bench. Wireless is different, y'can listen ter that an' get forward wi' job ...

VISITOR   How long have you been ... on your own?

OLD MAN   (*calculating mentally*) Well ... our lass were taken five years before I retired, so that's twenty odd years now.

VISITOR   You can't have looked forward to retiring – living on your own, I mean.

OLD MAN   (*philosophically*) Well, it took some gettin' used to; I missed the lads in the toolroom, we 'ad a few good laughs together, but I've allus kept a part of meself to meself, if yer see what I mean. I could allus live – 'ow shall I put it – in me own 'ead, if need be. That's where all this comes from, modellin' an' such, creatin' yer own world ...

Hiss of steam.

Kettle's boilin'!

VISITOR   Do you go back to the factory, ever?

OLD MAN   Well, I went back once or twice, but things change. Me old pals 'ad all gone – dead, a lot of 'em. An' works 'as been changin' fast in last few years. They got lathes now, yer just set 'em up an' put in a little card wi' instructions an' stand back – hey presto, job's done! Like automatic washin' machines. Very clever, fair play to fellers that design 'em an' build 'em, but it's not my idea o' craftsmanship, workin' a thing like that. 'Course, it's progress, but it's not fer me ... I don't know 'ow yer like yer tea, but it's 'ot an' strong down 'ere!

VISITOR   That's fine, thanks ... And these are your tools, on the bench ... To a technological ignoramus, like me, they're almost as fascinating as the models.

OLD MAN   Well, They're only basic, like; me scribes[2] an' files[3] an' callipers[4] an' punches[5] ... That little lathe I rigged up meself from base of our lass' old sewin' machine.

1 my wife   2 tools for scratching   3 smoothing   4 measuring   5 denting
metal

112

Slight clatter of metal as visitor picks things up.

VISITOR (*delightedly engrossed*) I thought this was a penknife, but it's got a kind of little metal fan at each end ...

OLD MAN (*bit anxiously*) That's me screw pitch gauges – metric one end, Whitworth t'other ...

Further faint clatter.

... And that's a die, fer cuttin' thread on bolts ... Could yer put 'em back where y'found 'em? ... A tool's no use if it's not in its place when y'want it!

VISITOR Sorry!

OLD MAN See, it's the 'andlin' o' these basic tools that's at the 'eart of engineerin' – that's why I wonder what lads are learnin' nowadays, wi' all this automation. Do they teach 'em basics o' workshop practice, like 'ow ter 'andle a file like this? It's an art, y'see, as well as a science. That's the idea o'craftsmanship, learnin' yer trade on the job. There's things can't be read in books, nor fed into computers ... In t' olden days, they used ter call a craft a *mystery*, an' there's a lot to that idea. Y'know, a tool like this file goes back, oh, thousands o' years, ter when men first worked wi' metals. Copper, then bronze, then iron – miners burrowin' underground, diggin' it up; an' smelters, turnin' ores into metal; an' smiths, changin' metal from one shape to another, one colour to another, hard to soft then back harder than before ... It were *magic*, lad – 'cos apart from magicians, priests an' suchlike, all t'other folk was just peasants, it'd be a miracle ter them, what metalworkers got up to – changin' bits o' the world. Think on it, lad ... Yon Greek god, Hephaestus, 'e were metal-worker on Olympus, they reckoned ... An' them old Assyrians, they wouldn't work metal wi'out a liberal supply o' the blood o'virgins ...

(*Chuckles, changing back to jocular mood*)

Assyrians wouldn't've got far in Sheffield, eh lad? Let's be gettin' on ...

VISITOR (*thoughtfully*) I think I'm beginning to understand the theme that runs through your work, your little captured moments of history ... They're all disasters which are *man-made*, examples of men's technological skill over-reaching[1] itself with calamitous results ... *Perhaps* because we've forgotten that technology has its roots in magic and mystery ...

OLD MAN   (*after long, baffled pause*) Aye, well, there's nowt so queer as folk[2]. What d'yer reckon to this?

VISITOR   Back to the sea again – a tug, what the name? – The *Grebecock* – and a submarine ... Is that a torpedo tube cover open, at the bows?

OLD MAN   (*delighted*) That's it! (*Serious*) When they dived someone opened t'other end of tube to inspect it. Front end sank like a brick an' stuck in seabed. June 1939, the *Thetis*, brand new T-class submarine just out of Birkenhead shipyard fer trials. 'Undred an' three on board, only four got out through escape apparatus ... 'Ad me work cut out finishin' that one on time – 1939, y'see, trade were pickin' up again in engineerin', wi' rearmament[3].

VISITOR   How do you mean, "on time"?

OLD MAN   (*oblivious*) ... Now compare that wi' this 'un ... More your time, this, y'might recall it.

VISITOR   Bigger submarine this time ... nuclear? And a naval surface ship ... *Skylark*. Yes, I remember this, the submarine was ... the *Thresher*, American navy, sank with all hands ...

OLD MAN   June 1963. First trial dive after a refit. Two 'undred odd miles off Cape Cod. Dived an' kept on goin' – eight thousand feet to the bottom – pressure plates were only built fer a thousand feet, maximum. 'Undred an' twenty nine aboard ... That were year I retired, 1963. They 'ad a little do, like; boss made a speech an' there were telegram from Group Chairman, whoever 'e might be ... They give us that clock in parlour, wi' inscription. Lads got together and give us yon socket set ... Anyway, bein' retired I could get to work full-time on yon *Thresher* model, ter get it finished fer June ...

VISITOR   ... But I thought you said the accident happened in June – that was when the submarine went down?

---

1 failing by attempting too much   **2** "there's nothing so odd as people" (Yorkshire saying)   **3** making new weapons for Second World War

OLD MAN (*as it is obvious*) Aye – hence the *urgency*.

VISITOR You mean you made the model *before* the thing happened?

OLD MAN (*a bit irritably*) That's what engineers make models *for* lad ... ter see 'ow things'll work out in practice – they're not *toys*.

(*Pause, then in more amiable tones*) I think we can squeeze another cup out o' pot ...

Sound of water pouring into teapot.

'Ow's time goin', lad?

VISITOR (*distracted – wondering if the Old Man is in fact senile*) Time ... Oh, sorry, it's, er, just coming up to one ...

OLD MAN I like ter catch news on t' wireless, keep up wi' what's 'appenin' ... Time enough to have tea, though. After I've caught 'eadlines, 'appen we could stroll down ter pub ...

VISITOR Yes, sure ... Um, you were kidding me, weren't you ...? About making the *Thresher* model before the accident?

OLD MAN (*more tolerantly than before*) Yer don't seem to 'ave grasped the principle, lad, I made 'em *all* before the thing 'appened; that's *why* it 'appened, as far as I can work it out. Started wi' *Titanic*, like I told yer, when I were an apprentice. I were fascinated, I read everythin' I could lay me 'ands on about it while it were buildin'. When I started model, I could *see*, some'ow, the way it ought ter be – all lit up at night, and great iceberg loomin' over it an' scrapin' alongside ... (*pause*) I used ter wonder if I ought ter feel bad about it, but it's not exactly me doin' it, yer see ... It's between me 'ands, and tools, an' materials I'm usin' ... I've 'eard yon primitive folk play 'ell wi' little dolls ter get at folk ... Well, us metal-workers ought ter be able ter manage a bit better magic than a bunch o' daft peasants, eh'? Mind you, there's no malice in it the way I do it, it just comes to me. I tried ringin' newspapers an' such ter give a bit o' warnin', but I give it up, it were floggin' a dead 'orse ... No sugar fer you, that right lad? Ee, I couldn't drink it wi'out me two spoonfuls ... 'Course, in me retirement I've managed ter get ahead of ...

Sound of spoon stirring tea.

... meself a bit ...

VISITOR Ahead of yourself ...?

OLD MAN Aye, I've got a few jobs laid out now, just waitin' fer finishin' touches ... (*Chuckles*) Enough ter see me out I should think ... 'Course I've 'ad ter learn a few new tricks – workin' wi' plastics an' so forth; an' supertankers, an' oil terminals ... Still, it's kept me on me toes. Feller that taught us at night school used ter 'ave a sayin', "Learnin' is livin'", 'e used ter say, an' there's a lot o' truth in that ...

VISITOR (*tentatively, beginning to believe*) What *exactly* have you got laid out?

OLD MAN (*mischieviously*) Ah well, that'd be tellin' wouldn't it ...? But I'll give yer clues ... There's some great 'eavy stuff goin' round in space, y'know – Skylab an' so forth, satellites – well, weight of 'em, an' orbits they're in, mean some 'ave got ter come down somewhere, sometime ... There'd be 'ell ter pay if I dropped one on Spaghetti Junction ...

VISITOR God Alminghat!

OLD MAN (*ruminatively*) I doubt it, lad – I must admit I wondered meself, early on; but I've come to the conclusion that I'm more likely playin' t'other side. I'll know soon, when whistle blows ... (*Chuckles*) 'Ave a look at this, though – what I finished this mornin'. I've 'ad it under this sheet. This is unveilin' like ... there:

VISITOR It's magnificent ... Definitely one of your best ... The guards at the gates, the alsations patrolling the electrified fences, little men in protective suits with geiger counters ...

OLD MAN It's a rum old business, atomic energy – I 'ad ter do some swottin' up ter get it all right. But I think it were worth it in' end. I'd draw yer attention ter the cut-away section of reactor[2] – yer can see right through ter core[3] – an' when I press this 'ere ...

---

1 multi-level road intersection outside Birmingham   2 apparatus for controlling and using the energy radiated by uranium   3 bundle of about 200 3.65 m × 20 cm (12′ × 8″) zircaloy rods containing pellets of uranium

Faint ominous hum.

... the control rods[1] start to draw out, an' reaction gets goin' ...

VISITOR   It's starting to glow ...

OLD MAN   I thought that were a nice fancy touch, makes a bit o'spectacle ... 'Course, if control rods jam too far out, y've got an uncontrolled reaction gettin' 'otter an' 'otter ...

VISITOR   (*panicking*) Is this building up to a nuclear explosion ...?

OLD MAN   (*chuckles*) Wi' mushroom cloud an' all trimmin's? Nay lad, not like that ... Just a bit o' fission[2] above what's wanted, an' 'appen no one notices till it's a bit late, an' they flood core wi' coolant – water in this case. But it's got too 'ot for that, an' coolant turns ter steam instantly an' expands, an' cracks open concrete shield ... an' then ye've got yer cloud of strontium[3] escapin' into atmosphere, an' then it all depends on prevailin' winds ...

VISITOR   ... This one's just completed?

OLD MAN   (*satisfied*) Aye. (*Pause*) Put wireless on, lad, Let's catch the news. An' the weather forecast.

---

1 rods of silver, cadmium and indium, which hinder the atomic reaction of uranium when they are inserted in the core   **2** atom-splitting   **3** strontium 90 – harmful radioactive fall-out

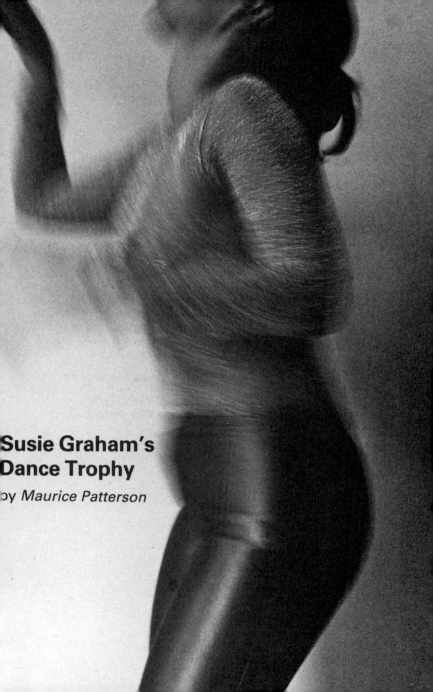

Susie Graham's Dance Trophy

by *Maurice Patterson*

The Cast

Susie *reserved and sullen, but effervescent in fantasy*
Mother *concerned, but uncomprehending*
Interviewer *well-known radio or TV personality*
Mason *Susie's imaginary partner*
Official *helpful careers adviser*
D.J. *well-known radio or TV personality*
Psychologist *female, efficient and sympathetic*
Police *constable*

Susie has only one thing to live for: her dream of being a champion disco-dancer. Her real life and her fantasy world grow further and further apart, despite her mother's efforts and much professional help.

The Official and Police can both be female and played by the same person.

Recorded sound effects are necessary for performance.

Susie Graham's Dance Trophy

1 Susie's bedroom

Disco music. Susie is dancing and making rhythmic sounds.

SUSIE   (*close on mic[1] – words only as a guide*)
Da da, da da da, da da, da da da; into – under – da
da da; round, round, round – la-la-la; da, da da da
da . . .

Sound of knocking from other side of bedroom door.

MOTHER   (*outside*) Susie – Susie, are you in there?

Music stops.

SUSIE   (*close on mic – still dancing*) Da, da da da etc. . . .
MOTHER   (*other side of door*) Susie! Will you answer me!!
SUSIE   (*silence for a second and then –*) What d'you want?
MOTHER   Don't you talk to your mother like that my girl!

Pause. Disco music starts to fade in, softly.

SUSIE   (*rhythmic*) One, two, one two three four – and round
. . .

MOTHER   (*other side of door*) Susie!

Music stops.

SUSIE   What?
MOTHER   I'm just starting dinner, love, so you can come down
and 'elp me.
SUSIE   Yeah, alright. In a minute.
MOTHER   (*receding*) There's a good girl now.
SUSIE   And then . . . find a super partner – competitions,
bigger and bigger competitions with my partner –
fantastic dancer called . . . called . . . Mason. Yeah,

---

1 microphone

Mason. Winning and winning with Mason and getting well-known.

Disco music in background.

Getting real well-known ... getting famous! And then, then there'd be the interviews –

Music gets louder and stops.

(*Close*) Dunno really – just the movement really. You know? You *feel* – yeah? Feel? It gets to you and – but you can't say the words for it – (*Slight laugh*) know what I mean?

INTERVIEW   (*a little away*) You mean the dancing says it for you?

SUSIE   (*close*) That's it. Well, you just start simple – I never meant to get into it like this. Then it sort of – gets you.

Slight pause.

I never really got – into anything before.

Loud music. Then applause. Music stops. D.J. starts to speak. His words are almost unintelligible – bad sound system, bad use of microphone. Words which should be heard are in capitals.

D. J.   So – a little SOLO DEMO BY SUSIE GRAHAM and MASON NACHANGI ends on a REAL HIGH NOTE which sets us up for your OWN D.J.'S NUMBER ONE CHOICE FOR THE WEEK.

Music gets louder and then fades into background.

SUSIE   You weren't with me Mason – not in the middle bit you weren't. You wasn't with me, you wasn't givin' nothin', Mason.

MASON   Susie, Susie baby; take it easy. Just relax; enjoy the thing. You know? It's for fun.

SUSIE   It's for real, Mason. You said we was going to work to win.

MASON   Sure baby – to win. A big, big silver trophy saying Mason and Susie are – the – very best!

1 demonstration

SUSIE GRAHAM'S DANCE TROPHY

SUSIE   Yeah that's right – the very best of all! Let's practise again Mason. Dance!

MASON   Again? I could use a drink, honey.

SUSIE   Dance, Mason. Come on, dance – dance – (*To the beat*) dance, dance – dance, dance, dance, dance –

Music stops.

INTERVIEW   Would you like to tell listeners about the costume you wear Susie?

SUSIE   (*close*) Well, me and my partner – Mason – we saved up and bought the gear – lurex satin. It was ever so dear, but when they judge you that all counts, see.

INTERVIEW   You have won competitions?

SUSIE   Oh yeah – only small ones yet though. I told Mason we'd got to go for this big one.

INTERVIEW   Is he your boyfriend?

SUSIE   Well – we're partners, aren't we? For the dancing I mean.

INTERVIEW   And what does your boyfriend think of all this?

SUSIE   (*quite violent*) What you on about? I ain't got no bloody boyfriend, 'ave I?

2 Office

MOTHER   Susie's never been able to stick at the jobs they've given 'er down the Job centre. 'Ave you Susie?

SUSIE   No.

OFFICIAL   Well, Susan, my job is to try and discover just exactly what type of work you're most suited for. There's nothing to worry about. Most young people take a little while to settle into the right sort of work. (*Slight pause*) I see you've left the space for hobbies and interests quite blank, Susan.

SUSIE   Yes.

OFFICIAL   No real interests of any kind? You see, Mrs Graham, a young person's hobbies can often give us a clue regarding career training.

MOTHER   She doesn't really take interest in anything much. Most the time she just sits; like she's miles away. When I ask 'er she says she's thinking. Day-dreaming, I call it.

OFFICIAL   I see. How about pop music? Most of you young people like pop music.

123

MOTHER   She 'ad a lovely music centre – Christmas – didn't you love? Up in 'er bedroom she 'as it. All fixed up like, with two of them loudspeakers, and knobs for this and knobs for that – wasn't cheap. But she never uses it. She don't do nothing really. Not really. Do you love?

SUSIE   Nothing to do is there?

Music loud. Then fade to acceptable background.

SUSIE   But I feel *with* you Mason. When it's good – then that's when it's like – you know – doing things *with* a person. Oh Mason, I don't think you know what I'm on about.

MASON   'S that right, honey? I don't know? How about this then? You mean – when you and I are working that routine you feel – linked up. You feel like we was having it away together[1].

SUSIE   No – no I don't mean that. That's not it – not that I'd know anyway 'cause we never 'ave. Mason, 'ow do you feel when it's finished?

MASON   The routine?

SUSIE   Yeah – 'ow do you feel?

MASON   I feel – hot, sticky, sweaty. Most often I have a thirst.

SUSIE   But don't you feel, like – good? High?

MASON   You're trying to work it all out, ain't you honey? Why don't you just take it? Want to try again?

The record draws to its close. Over it we hear the D. J.'s voice.

D. J.   (*over P.A.*[2] *as before*) And the non-stop disco show takes you right into THIS WEEK'S BIG CLIMBER IN THE CHARTS which, as the man said, NEEDS NO INTRODUCTION FROM ME . . .

Sound of new record.

SUSIE   Come on then Mason – we're going to do it. You and me, Mason, we're really going to do it.

---

1 making love   **2** Public Address system, loudspeaker

124

3 Psychologist's room

MOTHER   Susie filled in all those question forms, doctor – didn't you love?

PSYCHOL.   Yes – actually one isn't called 'doctor', Mrs Graham, I'm a psychologist as I explained to you before. Now Susan, you didn't answer a great number of the questions.

SUSIE   They seemed daft to me.

PSYCHOL.   It does seems to me, Susan, that there is no really great problem.

MOTHER   She's so withdrawn, doctor.

PSYCHOL.   Oh I'm not saying Susan has no difficulty. Many young people go through – phases of this sort. I think, Susan, that perhaps your complete lack of involvement in any interest, activity – even something quite simple can work.

SUSIE   I ain't got no interests.

PSYCHOL.   Hasn't there ever been something which caught your imagination so that you thought – now I'd really like to do that?

Slight pause.

SUSIE   'Ow do you mean?

Cut into town street scene: people etc. Establish then fade slightly.

INTERVIEW   I'm on the steps of the Bo-Down Disco entrance as people arrive for tonight's regional finals. Most of the young people are simply weekly disco dancers who have come to dance a few hours away and also watch the finals. Fourteen of them, however, are slightly nervous finalists. One couple is standing beside me right now. Hullo Susie.

SUSIE   Hullo

INTERVIEW   Susie Graham and I have chatted before on your local radio programme. Nervous Susie?

SUSIE   I'm excited – real excited.

INTERVIEW   How do you feel about getting this far?

SUSIE   Oh it's great. All this, interviews and that. Exciting. Then we get in the lights, all the gear on – my satin lurex gear – it's real then. Susie Graham, see?

4 Back in Susie's room

MOTHER   They just want to 'elp you Susie, that's all. That's all I want too – just to 'elp you.

SUSIE   I don't need no 'elp.

MOTHER   Oh you do, love. You're not going to tell me you like just sitting around, always in a dream, never going out, not meeting no one, not keeping yourself in work. I only wish I 'ad the chances you have when I was young.

SUSIE   What for?

MOTHER   What for? Well to make something of yourself. That's what that careers man was trying to do, wasn't he? I mean you just look at some of the girls you was at school with. All sorts of things they're doing now, some of them – hairdressing an' that. All sorts.

SUSIE   I'm alright.

MOTHER   You're not alright. You make me cross sometimes, Susie, you do really. I wouldn't mind so much if you seemed to care about it all. But it don't seem to bother you that you're wasting your life away. Trouble is with you, love, you've got no ambition.

Music.

INTERVIEW   Well you and Mason are next, Susie. How do you rate the opposition?

SUSIE   What, the others? Oh we're best.

INTERVIEW   Well, listeners, there you have it; complete confidence from Susie Graham.

SUSIE   'Cause when you look at the others you can tell the difference, see.

INTERVIEW   Great Susie. Well now I'm going to chat to –

SUSIE   They're not like us. Some of 'em like the dancing and some of 'em want the winning, but I'm both. Like it, want it, love it – living it. Me and this bloke – together see? Doing it well and doing it best. Winning it. Then when it's done – when it's done, we've done it and it's like a big round bell you can get hold of. And it's always, always going to be just like this. Just always.

Disco music gets louder. Applause over music.

5 Living room of small house

MOTHER (*a little away*) You want to cut out some of those cakes and stuff, Susie. You're putting on weight you know.

SUSIE (*close*) I'm hungry.

MOTHER Oh you can't be, love. You only 'ad your big dinner half an hour ago. We'll 'ave to put you on one of them diets if you're not careful.

SUSIE Anyway, I like cakes.

MOTHER Well you certainly enjoy your food, I'll say that for you. I said to that doctor – whatever she was called – I said well, at least she enjoys 'er food.

SUSIE What's for supper?

MOTHER Why don't you go and put some of your records on, love? Some of your new top twenty I got you.

SUSIE I don't wanna play records; I'm bored with them.

MOTHER You're a funny girl, you really are. I don't know why you don't ever go out a bit more. Pretty girl like you – should 'ave lots of boyfriends taking you out and everything.

SUSIE Don't see why.

MOTHER Don't see why? Well 'cause it's only natural, that's why.

SUSIE Well they don't, so that's it ain't it?

MOTHER You don't 'ave to snap at your mum, love. 'Ave you 'ad one of your tablets tonight?

SUSIE I don't like them; they make me feel funny.

MOTHER Oh, Susie, they're supposed to make you feel better; that's why the lady doctor gave them to you.

SUSIE Well they don't make me feel better. They make me feel 'orrible. So why – so why go on about bloody boyfriends!

MOTHER Susie!

Sound of applause which starts to die down.

INTERVIEW Thank you Frank and Jenny. Which brings us to the final contestants in this final show. Ladies and gentlemen – Susie Graham and Mason Nachangi!

Slight applause: music starts.

SUSIE (*close, over music*) This is what it's like – at the actual final; where we've got to – I've got to. It just all goes so easy, the moving is so easy – and after a bit we're so good they start clapping, and that, when it's only half-way through.

Burst of applause over music. Then – during the next speech – Slow cross fade to open-air acoustic: country sounds, birds etc.

I can do it. There's some posh geezer waiting to give that silver prize thing at the end. And nobody even told me how – just did it with no learning or nothin' – just being best 'cause I'm Susie and they are saying I'm best. It's only a start though, 'cause there's bigger ones to win – must be. And that's what got me known – lots of money in it if you're right up top.

But I'm glad I took Mason. I'd 'ave felt bad if I'd dropped him. That's it – all the way with Mason. 'E'll get money too 'cause we're partners. So he took me in his new car – trust 'im to get a flash one – right out in the country. All fresh and birds and that; and he talked to me real nice – didn't you Mason? Mason! Where the 'ell are you, Mason!?

Music still loud.

MASON   Right here, Susie baby. We're going just great!
SUSIE   Mason I –
MASON   It's the big ending Susie. Big – that's it!!

Music gets louder – applause starts. Then cut to house interior.

MOTHER   Are you sitting there sulking, love? (*Pause*) Silly to sulk. And you know I never can abide you swearing in the 'ouse. That's why I shouted a bit. Come on, love – cheer up now.
SUSIE   I'm not sulking.
MOTHER   Well I don't know what you are doing then. Just sitting saying nothing – staring at the telly and it's not even on.
SUSIE   I'm thinking, ain't I?
MOTHER   Why don't you put the telly on if you're going to stare at it?
SUSIE   Nothing on.

MOTHER	Well, if all you can do with your Saturday evening is sit and stare, the best thing for you is an early night. You're looking a bit peeky anyway.
SUSIE	Alright.
MOTHER	Eh?
SUSIE	Alright – I'll go to bed then.
MOTHER	Oh. Well wouldn't you like some supper first? Susie? Isn't there – anything you want love?

No music. Dying applause.

INTERVIEW	So our congratulations to the outright winners of this competition. Yes, indeed, it's Susie Graham and Mason Nachangi!

Applause.

	And the *very* happy and smiling couple are collecting their trophy right now. If I can just get a word with them ... Susie, Mason? So what does it feel like?
SUSIE	It feels – real great. Like – we've won and ... and ...
INTERVIEW	I think the little girl is a bit overcome just now. Mason, is this the peak, or is it just a beginning?
MASON	Yeah, well I've got a great partner here, so I don't see any reason to stop now. How about you, Susie honey?
SUSIE	Me? I dunno much further than this bit – except for your car – and fields and that – and there should be some birds singing – and feeling sort of ... loose inside of me – I dunno much more than that ...
INTERVIEW	Right on Susie! And with those few – thoughtful – words from winner Susie Graham, we're going to ask our resident D. J. Johny Westland, to spin that disc again so our winners can do their own – lap of honour!

Music starts.

Ladies and gentlemen – Mason and Susie!

Applause, music. At same time echo Interviewer's 'Susie' and then – over applause and music and taking over from echo.

MOTHER	(*a scream*) Susie!! (*Crying*) Susie Girlie, why? Why?

Inside the house.

POLICE Not by mistake Mrs Graham – even young girls don't take a whole bottle of tablets by mistake.

MOTHER But she wouldn't kill 'erself, officer. Why should she?

POLICE There was no note? Nothing at all – just the empty bottle?

MOTHER And the dress – the dress she was clutching.

POLICE *Her* dress?

MOTHER Well no – that is, not really. She wouldn't wear a thing like that – all lurex and satin an' that – not our Susie. It was one she brought 'ome – about a month ago – got it up the OXFAM[1] she said. Well you can see – it's all torn anyway – she couldn't 'ave worn it. I told 'er – you're a funny girl Susie, I said. What you want to spend your money on an old thing like that? But she seemed to like it –

Fade in background of open-air sounds: bird song etc. Over this the sound of Susie quietly humming one of the disco tunes.

She never tried to mend it or nothin' – funny girl. (*Slight pause*) I mean, what did she *want*? That's what I could never work out. (*Slight pause*) Whatever did she want?

Sound of birds in the distance and Susie humming slightly.

---

1 charity shop run by the Oxford Committee for Famine Relief

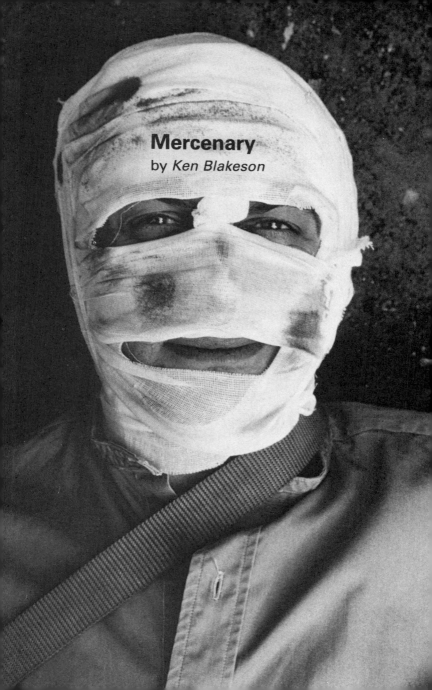

Mercenary
by *Ken Blakeson*

The Cast

Buller *a middle-aged white mercenary*
Elliot *a young English ambulance driver*
Officer *a black African liberation leader*

In a war-torn African state, the neutral Elliot is forced to aid the professional fighter Buller. Neither is personally involved in the war, but they have both chosen to risk their lives: one to take, and one to save, the lives of others.

Recorded sound effects are necessary for performance.

Mercenary

1 Africa

The sound of crickets chirping. An ambulance approaches from the distance. As it gets nearer there is a burst of automatic fire from an F.N. rifle[1]. The sudden noise shatters the peace. The crickets are silent. Sound of glass breaking in the side window of the ambulance, which pulls up noisily and ticks over. Buller runs from cover and hammers on the door.

BULLER   Out!

He wrenches the door open.

     Switch the motor off. Let's see those hands! (*His voice is tense but commanding*) Move it! Move it

ELLIOT   Don't shoot. I'm neutral. Relief Organisation!

He jumps out of cab.

     Don't shoot. I'm Elliot. Here's my papers.

BULLER   Spread yourself!

He frisks Elliot.

ELLIOT   We don't carry weapons.

BULLER   Keys! Give me the keys!

ELLIOT   I can't. I've got to pick up some men ...

Buller punches him in the stomach. Elliot retches.

     Ughh!

BULLER   I said keys!

Elliot coughs painfully.

ELLIOT   There was no need ... no need ...

He coughs again, then throws the keys over to Buller.

---

1   standard NATO issue weapon

BULLER   You being British makes no difference to me, boy[1].

ELLIOT   What are you doing?

BULLER   I'm taking your ambulance.

ELLIOT   Please . . . it's needed.

BULLER   That's right. I need it. Now, over there.

ELLIOT   But it belongs to the relief organisation.

BULLER   Did! Belongs to me now. Now shut it! Right, my little do gooder . . . we've got a choice. This . . .

He cocks rifle.

. . . or you drive to Kinsenghi.

ELLIOT   I've got to pick up some wounded men in M'Bala.

BULLER   You're wasting my time, boy.

ELLIOT   They'll die if I don't get them to the hospital.

BULLER   Too bad.

ELLIOT   You're a mercenary, aren't you?

BULLER   Now I wonder how you guessed that. Right, stop friggin' about. I just haven't got the time.

ELLIOT   You haven't got a chance.

BULLER   Nothing lost then is there? I've been waiting all day for one of these.

He bangs the side of the ambulance.

Even the Liberationists won't shoot up an ambulance. Now come on sunshine, either drive me or I'll give it to you right where you stand.

ELLIOT   (*calm*) You're not going to kill me.

BULLER   Listen, you'd be dead now if you hadn't had a white skin. Just get lucky.

ELLIOT   What about the wounded men I'm supposed to pick up?

BULLER   What do I care.

ELLIOT   Some of them are from your side.

BULLER   I'm on my own side, boy.

ELLIOT   You know there's liberationists in Kinsenghi?

BULLER   And an airfield.

ELLIOT   It's guarded.

Buller pulls out currency.

---

1 used to address a (black) servant.

BULLER   See that Elliot ... That's money! That buys all loyalties.

ELLIOT   I know you ... You're Buller.

BULLER   Yes I'm the Fairy Snowman and this is your star prize ... Now are you in ... or right out?

ELLIOT   What choice have I?

BULLER   Well ... I don't want to make things complicated for you.

ELLIOT   I'll need the keys.

BULLER   When we're both inside that cab ... Not that side ... this. I don't want to lose you do I? Not after waiting all day. Come on ... move it ...

Elliot climbs in, followed by Buller. We are now in the cab with them. Buller shuts the cab door.

Right then, nice and steady. We don't want to draw attention to ourselves, do we? Let's go.

Elliot starts the motor. It ticks over.

ELLIOT   You realise you're killing those men at M'Bala.

BULLER   A few more won't make any difference. Let's go.

Engine revs and departs. Fade.

2 Cab interior

Constant engine sound.

ELLIOT   You don't say very much.

BULLER   I'm thinking.

ELLIOT   Have you thought of giving yourself up? The whole country's overrun now.

BULLER   You must be joking.

ELLIOT   At least you'll stay alive.

BULLER   Just long enough to be a side show.

ELLIOT   Side show?

BULLER   Pin the ears back on the mercenary[1]!

ELLIOT   They wouldn't do that.

BULLER   Oh no. Of course, I forgot ... the Geneva Convention[2]. I feel safe now.

---

1 Buller suggests his captors will cut off his ears for amusement   **2** international agreements on the treatment of prisoners, wounded and dead in war

ELLIOT   Look I know you're not protected by the convention, but they are human beings.

BULLER   Have you ever seen what they do to mercenaries?

ELLIOT   No ...

BULLER   Then you're a very lucky man. Oh they keep them alive all right ... just. And there is a certain degree of pain involved in the process.

ELLIOT   They're not like that. I know them. They've always helped me.

BULLER   Well they would do, wouldn't they? I mean you patch up their soldiers ... the ones I shoot.

ELLIOT   We make no distinction between sides. We help everybody.

BULLER   Very noble. Still, you're helping me now eh?

ELLIOT   Not through choice. I've nothing in common with you.

BULLER   Except colour. We're both white men.

ELLIOT   What's colour got to do with it?

BULLER   Everything boy. Haven't you discovered yet? They're animals ... kids ... both sides! The only professionals out here are the white men. The mercs. When we've gone there'll be nobody.

ELLIOT   They can do without your sort of help.

BULLER   (*cheerful*) What you trying to do? Deny me a living?

ELLIOT   You don't have to do it.

BULLER   Oh but I do ... and I get well paid for it. Here ... slow down a bit. Don't get carried away.

ELLIOT   How can you kill people for money?

BULLER   I once had a mate worked in a cigarette factory ... Think about it.

ELLIOT   But people choose to smoke. You don't discriminate when you pull a trigger.

BULLER   Yeah ... and it's legal. Like polluting rivers and poisoning the air. Still that's all right, isn't it? That's acceptable.

ELLIOT   That's no argument and you know it. Two wrongs don't make a right.

BULLER   Listen son ... it's survival we're talking about. That's all. Now there's politicians all over this tin-pot country with high-sounding words, lining their pockets[1] every day ... filling up and getting out! The whole bloody

---

1 taking bribes

lot of 'em are looting, killing, raping ... They've never had it so good ... so why pick on me?

ELLIOT Because you know there's a better way.

BULLER For some ...

ELLIOT And the kids ... the ones with arms and legs missing ... the orphans ...

BULLER I didn't start this war.

ELLIOT Have you seen the kids, Buller? The ones you kill and maim?

BULLER Yeah ... I've seen the kids ... I've seen them come at me with Kalashnikov rifles[1] ... so don't give me any of that brotherhood of man crap.

ELLIOT How many children have you killed Buller?

BULLER I kill soldiers ... terrorists. Not kids. Ask the liberationists. They burn the villages down.

ELLIOT But that's the point, don't you see? If there were no sides there'd be no war, no suffering.

BULLER Listen boy. Jesus Christ couldn't change human nature so don't flatter yourself.

ELLIOT You'll never see will you?

BULLER Oh I see all right. I see things my way. The way I've learned to see. The way people like you've taught me. Now shut up and drive.

(*Pause*)

ELLIOT How old are you, Buller?

BULLER Forty three.

ELLIOT You're older than the rest.

BULLER Yeah ... I'm good at my job. Only good mercenaries grow old.

ELLIOT What about the young ones?

BULLER What about them?

ELLIOT Why do they do it?

BULLER Ask them.

ELLIOT Excitement? Money? Liven up dull lives?

BULLER (*thoughtfully*) Yeah ... that's part of it.

ELLIOT (*angry*) You call that a reason?!

BULLER You're really full of yourself, aren't you? What is it? ... No. Let me guess. 'A' levels, University Voluntary Service Overseas ... Out to save Mankind.

1 Russian firearms popular with terrorists and mercenaries

ELLIOT So?

Buller lights a fag.

BULLER You've had it easy, boy.

ELLIOT How do you know?

Buller blows out smoke.

BULLER Take my lads. My young killers ... what's left of them ...

ELLIOT You take them Buller. They're yours.

BULLER Now hang on. You've had your say. Take my boys ... they're fifteen, right? They're sitting at home watching telly, dying to leave school and they're not too bright. Average to thick, right? Lower than average prospects. Suddenly the screen flickers and there's some kid who's hardly started shaving, skiing down some romantic Swiss Alp ... chatting up the sort of bird you'd find at a Hollyood premiere ... dressed in combat gear, handling a beautiful expensive S.L.R.[1] ... travelling round the world and being paid. He's a professional! This spotty-faced kid who last week had no horizons past the fish and chip shop is a professional! Not a yob mind. (*He pauses*)

A professional! So, all my lads aged fifteen think to themselves in front of the telly ... Here, let's have some of that! and what do they do? ... They join Her Majesty's armed forces. They meet men like me who fitten them up, teach them to kill efficiently and effectively, help them find their way round with a soldering iron and send them to Northern Ireland. Maybe one or two trips and before they know where they are, they're twenty two and three and they've got a chance to get out ... and suddenly it strikes them ... They've never seen a pair of skis ... they've never met any randy starlets. They realise Catterick[2], Aldershot[3] and Northern Ireland[4] aren't really Switzerland or the South of France and they say stuff this for a lark and leave. They get jobs, some of them or they hang around the depots, chatting to old mates.

1 Self-Loading Rifle 2 army training camp in North Yorkshire 3 main British army base in Hampshire 4 main active service posting

But some settle to civvy life and others go off their skull with boredom. They're big fit lads ... trained to kill ... experts humping bricks[1] ... And suddenly they realise they're not professionals any more so they look round ... drift a bit ... see an advert and bingo! ... next stop Africa.

ELLIOT But surely there are schemes ... government centres ...

BULLER Schemes are the last thing these men need.

ELLIOT Did that happen to you?

BULLER That's another story altogether.

Silence.

ELLIOT Would you really have killed me back there on the road?

BULLER What do you think?

ELLIOT I don't think you would.

BULLER Then you'd be wrong.

ELLIOT Do you enjoy killing?

BULLER It's part of the job. I do it if it's necessary.

ELLIOT I feel sorry for you.

BULLER That's why you're on the other end of this rifle, son.

ELLIOT I never want to be on your end of it.

BULLER You don't need to be do you? I mean you've got brains, opportunities. I didn't have those luxuries at your age.

ELLIOT You're intelligent. You don't have to do it now.

BULLER Too late now. What does an ex-sergeant instructor from the paras do when he leaves? I had men under me boy ... I had a position. Respect. Now can you see me opening lift doors showing off me medals or driving round in a tin truck protecting other people's gelt[2] for fifty quid a week? You see, like it or not, I am an expert. An expert in the art of warfare and that gives me some standing. People are prepared to pay well for my expertise and give me the respect I think I'm due. You can't ask a man to give up his self-respect now can you?

Elliot does not answer for a while.

ELLIOT We'll be coming to the Kinsenghi–M'Bala intersection in a while.

---

1 skilled men doing unskilled labour   **2** Dutch for money

BULLER Just take the Kinsenghi Road.

ELLIOT There might be a roadblock.

BULLER How far off are we?

ELLIOT About two miles. Look, wouldn't you stand a better chance on foot? If there is a roadblock there'll be liberationist troops ...

BULLER You can't wait to get to those wounded heroes, can you?

ELLIOT They need attention and what chance have you got at a roadblock? We'll all die if they find you. It's a waste.

BULLER Is there no way round the block?

ELLIOT No.

BULLER Pull off the road. Behind those trees ...

ELLIOT What are you going to do?

BULLER Just do as I say. Pull off ... You're going to fix me up.

Elliot pulls the ambulance off the road and switches off the ignition.

Right. Break out the bandages.

ELLIOT Bandages?

BULLER That's right. I'm going to be a patient. A black liberationist who's copped a land mine ...

ELLIOT We won't get away with that.

BULLER We'd better or there'll be a lot of of dead men floating about ... including you.

ELLIOT But there's no hospital at M'Bala.

BULLER I'm a critical case. I need immediate attention at Kinsenghi hospital.

ELLIOT But they'll check. They'll look in the back.

BULLER And they'll find me covered in bandages unable to speak.

ELLIOT It won't work Buller.

BULLER Get cracking. We're wasting time ...

Fade.

3 Inside the back of the ambulance

BULLER Plenty round the face. Leave the mouth and eyes ... How do I look?

ELLIOT Like the Invisible Man.

BULLER I wish I was ... Right. Blood!

ELLIOT Blood?

BULLER   Blood! You must carry it.

ELLIOT   Yes, but it's scarce. We don't have enough.

BULLER   Enough for what I need. Get it.

ELLIOT   On the right.

Buller grabs bottle and smashes it.

BULLER   Put some on the face and the chest. Don't spare it. I want this to look right.

ELLIOT   This could have saved someone's life.

BULLER   Let's hope it's mine. Right. In the cab. That'll have to do. And remember if you're stopped I've got this rifle pointed at your head.

ELLIOT   What if they want papers?

BULLER   I've got papers. Papers for every occasion. I told you ... I'm a professional.

ELLIOT   It won't work ... Give yourself up. I'll help. I know some of the junior officers ... they were educated in British Universities ... They're intelligent men ...

BULLER   They wouldn't like me then, would they? Just drive ... and remember the rifle.

Sound of engine starting and ambulance driving off.

4 On the road again

Sound of ambulance engine slowing down.

ELLIOT   We're approaching the intersection. There's a roadblock!

BULLER   Right, pull up nice and slowly. How many soldiers?

ELLIOT   A dozen. All armed.

BULLER   Just keep calm. Do as I told you.

ELLIOT   They're signalling me to stop.

BULLER   So stop! Don't do anything to arouse suspicion.

ELLIOT   They want me to get out of the cab.

BULLER   Just sit tight.

ELLIOT   Look I'll have to get out. They'll think it's funny if I stay in.

BULLER   Nice and steady then. And don't forget. The rifle's on your head Elliot.

ELLIOT   I won't shop you Buller.

BULLER   You'd better not.

ELLIOT   Get down, you fool. I'm going out.

He opens cab door.

ELLIOT (*shouts*) My name's Elliot. International Relief Organisation. I've got a man in the back who needs immediate treatment at Kinsenghi Hospital. Here's my papers.

He jumps down.

OFFICER (*cultured voice*) Mr Elliot! Is the man ours or theirs?

ELLIOT Yours . . . He's badly wounded. A mine, I think.

OFFICER We shall take a look at him . . . please.

ELLIOT Of course. But please . . . don't delay . . .

Officer walks to back of ambulance.

OFFICER Have you seen signs of enemy activity on the road, Mr Elliot?

ELLIOT I'm a driver for a neutral organisation, lieutenant. I can't answer that.

OFFICER It is for your sake I ask. You are of great use to us and we value your help.

ELLIOT Both sides are served lieutenant. They're just injured people to me.

OFFICER There are still small bands of mercenaries moving towards Kinsenghi. They will make for the airport . . . try to bribe their way out. They really are silly, Mr Elliot. We have all exits guarded.

ELLIOT Why are you telling me all this?

OFFICER They are dangerous men, Mr Elliot. Like trapped rats, they will leap for the throat. They kill for money not for justice.

Elliot opens the doors at the back of the ambulance.

ELLIOT All killing is wasteful.

OFFICER Maybe so . . . maybe . . . This is the man?

ELLIOT Yes.

OFFICER Let me see.

The officer climbs into the ambulance. Atmosphere changes.

Will he live?

ELLIOT That depends on how long you keep me here. He's lost a lot of blood.

OFFICER We have many men like this, Mr Elliot.

The officer walks out into the open air again.

Please. Close the doors. We will not slow you down. (*Shouts*) Raise the pole!

ELLIOT Thank you.

Elliot climbs into cab.

OFFICER Take care, Mr Elliot. This country needs men like you.

ELLIOT Thank you.

He starts the motor.

BULLER (*hisses*) Good boy ... now steady ... don't cock it up now ...

ELLIOT Hang on ... the officer's waving me down again.

BULLER Christ, he's realised!

Buller cocks the rifle.

ELLIOT No ... no ... get back down. He's pointing to the rear wheel. Stay down Buller. I'll see what he wants.

BULLER Be quick!

Elliot opens door and jumps out.

OFFICER Your rear tyre, Mr Elliot. It's very thin.

ELLIOT Yes. I'll change it at Kinsenghi.

OFFICER You will find nothing much there. I have spares which should fit. Come ... I'll give you one ... over here in my truck ...

They walk away.

(*Lowering his voice*) Just keep walking, Mr Elliot. Do not arouse his suspicions. He has a gun on you?

ELLIOT A gun? Who?

OFFICER It is useless to try to save him, Mr Elliot. Believe me. I trust you did not help him voluntarily?

ELLIOT No.

OFFICER I have no wish to harm you. That is why I got you out of the ambulance.

ELLIOT How did you know. I mean all the bandages ... The blood.

OFFICER His eyes, Mr Elliot.

ELLIOT His eyes?

OFFICER Only Europeans have blue eyes ... not black men. In

this country the only Europeans left are men like yourself and mercenaries. He is a mercenary, isn't he?

ELLIOT He's afraid you'll torture him.

OFFICER He needn't be ... Corporal. Now!

Burst of light machine gun fire. It rips into the rear bodywork of the ambulance.

ELLIOT (*shocked*) No ... no ...

OFFICER I can take no chances. I'm sorry about your ambulance.

ELLIOT No ...

Runs to ambulance and opens rear doors.

Buller! Buller!

The officer joins him.

OFFICER He's dead, Mr Elliot. Still we have only damaged the bodywork of your ambulance. You! You! Get him out!

ELLIOT He's dead!

OFFICER You can be on your way now. We will not bother you. Don't feel sorry for him, Mr Elliot. He's just scum ... See blue eyes ... as I said. Blue eyes. They see nothing now, Mr Elliot.

ELLIOT No ... (*Sighs*) Then perhaps they never did. Perhaps they never did.

The Bognor Regis Vampire

by *J. C. W. Brook*

The Cast

Agnes *Rodney's unflappable lady wife*
Rodney *a retired major*
Bert *a reluctantly bloodthirsty vampire*
Hilda *the maid, accustomed to unusual duties*

The major and his wife live in an isolated house overlooking the cemetery. It is just before midnight on the night of the full moon, and the Council has been disturbing an ominously inscribed tomb. Rodney and Agnes are oddly undisconcerted when an unexpected caller kills their butler and threatens their lives.

The Bognor Regis Vampire

Distant night-time noises. Agnes turns a page of the newspaper.

AGNES   (*reading newspaper*) I see the borough council is rebuilding the graveyard, Rodney.

RODNEY   (*over by open window*) Ummm?

AGNES   I saw it from my bedroom window. That hideous vault in the corner's been flattened.

RODNEY   Really? That one with the mysterious inscription over the door? How does it go? "Disturb me not or the blood will flow, remove the stake and my fangs will grow", that one, you mean?

AGNES   Yes dear.

RODNEY   Vandals.

Ting ting ting of carriage clock striking the quarter to.

AGNES   A quarter to, dear. You'd better close the window.

RODNEY   Just looking at the moon.

Agnes puts paper down, stands, moves, joins him.

AGNES   Even so, we don't want to take more chances than need be with your old complaint.

RODNEY   Yes, dear.

AGNES   Oh, just look at the way the mist's curling about the garden gnomes.

RODNEY   (*snorts depreciatingly*) Haa!

AGNES   Gnomes, Rodney, are de rigeur[1] in Bognor.

A fluttering is heard, getting closer.

AGNES   Gracious me, what's that?

RODNEY   Just a bat, dear.

Bat now close – squeaks.

---

1 compulsory because of the fashion

AGNES   A bat? But Rodney, it must be at least a yard across.

RODNEY   So it is. David Attenborough's got a lot to answer for.

Bat flaps away.

AGNES   Oh, it's gone round the side of the house. Never mind. I'll just close the window.

She does so. Rodney moves away and sits.

RODNEY   I wish Jarvis would hurry with the port.

Rusty and ancient doorbell rings, deep in interior of house.

AGNES   Oh! Visitors.

RODNEY   Llewellyn, I expect.

AGNES   No. He's never early.

A long gurgling blood-curdling scream is heard, off.

Oh!

RODNEY   I say, what was that? Your tummy again, Agnes?

AGNES   It was not my tummy, Rodney.

She moves.

It came from the hall. I shall investigate.

RODNEY   If you must.

AGNES   Just a little peek ...

She opens the door.

Oh!

RODNEY   What is it, Agnes?

AGNES   It's Jarvis, dear. He's lying on the hall floor. I think he's dead.

RODNEY   Dead?

AGNES   Dead. Quite white.

RODNEY   Damned inconsiderate of him. You'll have to get Hilda to fetch the port.

AGNES   He's not alone, dear.

RODNEY   Oh?

AGNES   There's a young man bending over him, and ... oh Rodney, there's blood coming from Jarvis's neck.

RODNEY   Blood?

AGNES   Blood.

Rodney joins her.

148

RODNEY Let me see ... I say, you're right Agnes.

A sort of obscene licking/sucking noise can be heard coming from the hall.

AGNES Is that young man an acquaintance of yours, Rodney?

RODNEY Certainly not. He looks distinctly scruffy.

AGNES What peculiar teeth he has.

RODNEY Teeth or no teeth, I'm going to ask him what he's doing.

He moves into hall.

I say – I say – you there – excuse me.

Licking/sucking noise stops.

BERT Ummm?

RODNEY What do you think you're doing, eh?

Bert stands up.

BERT Er ... erm ...

AGNES Rodney – he's got blood round his mouth.

RODNEY (*perceptively*) There's something deuced odd going on here, Agnes.

Bert moves near to them.

BERT Sorry if I startled you. Bertram Tomkiss at your service. How do you do?

AGNES How do you do? Oh, your hand is so cold.

BERT Sorry – part of my condition, y'know.

AGNES I am Mrs Sloan, and this is my husband, Major Rodney Sloan.

RODNEY Late of the Buffs[1]. How d'you do?

BERT Pleased to meet you, I'm sure.

RODNEY You're right, Agnes – cold as the grave.

AGNES Perhaps, Mr Tomkiss, you would care to explain what you've done with Jarvis.

BERT Jarvis?

RODNEY Our butler, sir.

BERT Oh ... erm ... him. I was hoping you'd have forgotten. I've killed him, sort of.

1 retired from the East Kent Regiment

RODNEY   Killed him? That's taking a bit of a liberty, isn't it?

BERT   Yes, well, I'm sorry about that, but transformations take a lot out of one, and I'd collided with a yew tree on the way here – I can never get the hang of navigation by radar. I only stopped by to ask the way to the nearest YWCA[1], as it happens, when he opened the door. I saw his jugular vein pulsing away above his starched collar and just thought "breakfast" and jumped. I'm terribly sorry if it's going to cause you any inconvenience.

(Slight pause)

AGNES   Perhaps you'd care to go into the living room, Mr Tomkiss, and warm yourself by the fire.

BERT   That's very civil of you. Thank you . . .

He exits to the living room.

RODNEY   *(lowering voice)* Dammit, Agnes, this chappie comes in here without so much as a by-your-leave and kills Jarvis. For all you know he could be an undesirable character. Are you sure you should invite him into the living room?

AGNES   I know what I am doing, Rodney.

She enters the living room.

That's right, Mr Tomkiss – do make yourself comfortable. Tell me – d'you like port[2]?

BERT   As long as it's red, yes please.

AGNES   I shall ring for Jarvis to – oh, silly me. Hilda will have to bring it.

Tinkle tinkle of bell.

My husband often likes a little nip at this time of night. Do stop prowling, Rodney, and sit down.

Rodney sits.

RODNEY   Sorry dear.

BERT   Erm . . . did you say Hilda?

---

1 Young Women's Christian Association – all-female hostel   **2** sweet, strong Portuguese wine – red, white or tawny

AGNES   Our maid, Mr Tomkiss – a nice young girl from the orphanage.

BERT   (*being overcome by blood lust*) Young? How young?

AGNES   She is eighteen, I believe.

BERT   Has she got creamy white skin and a heaving bosom and a palpitating neck and long black hair I can twine my fingers round as I bend her head back to expose her throat so I can sink my ... (*Has been slowing, stops*)

AGNES   Are you feeling quite all right, Mr Tomkiss? You were quivering for a while there.

BERT   Yes, yes, yes ... erm ... sorry.

Opening of door. Hilda enters.

HILDA   You rang, madam?

BERT   Ohhhhh – eight full pints or I'm a Dutchman.

AGNES   Yes Hilda – could you bring the port?

HILDA   Yes, madam.

RODNEY   Two glasses, m'dear.

HILDA   Sir ...

She moves. Stops.

Er ... sir, madam – Jarvis is in the hall, and I think he's dead. I wasn't sure if you knew.

AGNES   Yes, we had noticed, thank you.

HILDA   Yes madam ... thank you ...

She exits.

BERT   Ohhhhh, what a specimen – makes my fangs go whang.

RODNEY   Yes, she certainly is a well-built little filly.

AGNES   Rodney!

RODNEY   Sorry dear.

AGNES   Mr Tomkiss, I don't want to appear unduly inquisitive, but what exactly do you do?

BERT   Er ... do?

AGNES   Forgive me for being personal, but you have several peculiarities my husband and I can't help remarking on. Your teeth. Your bloodstained shirt-front. Your white face and staring red eyes. The length of your fingernails. The coldness of your skin and the fact that our mahogany mirror over the fireplace seems to ignore your existence.

BERT   Oh, why is it people always see straight through me?

151

Oh well, I suppose I'll have to own up sometime. I'm a vampire.

RODNEY   A vampire?

BERT   I drink people's blood for a dying. Oh – not from choice, mind you – mum was got at by a bat when she was on a package holiday in Transylvania[1]. Went walking in the forest at night – all the locals tried to make her carry a bit of garlic . . .

RODNEY   Garlic? Ergh – foreign muck. Give me curry any day.

BERT   Anyway, off into the forest she went, thinking she might find some mushrooms, when this giant bat swooped down from a nearby schloss[2] and carried her off to the nearest gooseberry bush. She said it was the most bizarre experience of her life, and I can well imagine it. Being raped by a bat when all you had been thinking about was edible fungi isn't exactly a normal way of passing an evening – oh, I'm sorry Mrs Sloan, to erm . . .

AGNES   Oh, don't mind me, Mr Tomkiss – pray continue. I find this most fascinating.

RODNEY   To tell the truth the old memsahib[3] likes a bit of racy talk now and again – listens to 'The Archers' every day.

BERT   Well, in the due course of time along I came – a perfectly normal kid – went to school and everything, when – on my eighteenth birthday – at midnight – bang – out came these two enormous teeth. You can imagine how startled I was – by Jove, I thought, something's odd here. I then changed into a bat and zoomed out of the window. Ended up clinging to the top of Frinton town hall feeling sick with vertigo.

AGNES   Oh, you poor man.

BERT   It's not much use being a bat if you can't stand heights. And then the clock struck one and I fell off – right on top of a lady of easy virtue[4] passing by below. I shall spare you the gory details, but she tasted rather nice. I've had a liking for A Positive ever since. Mind you – after I'd dumped her body off the nearest cliff I couldn't help feeling rather ashamed of myself – mother had

---

1 scenic central province of Rumania   **2** small German castle   **3** Hindi for ma'am – the major has served in India   **4** prostitute

always told me to stay clear of scarlet women, gambling and patent leather[1] shoes. Up until then I'd always wanted to be a conscientious objector[2].

Door opens. Hilda enters with tray.

HILDA The port, sir.

BERT Ohhhhh ...

RODNEY Thank you, Hilda.

HILDA Sir ...

She puts the tray down.

Will there be anything else?

AGNES Yes, Hilda. Now that Jarvis is no longer with us we shall expect you to undertake his duties – until, that is, we can find someone else. You understand?

HILDA Yes madam, perfectly.

BERT Ermmm ...?

HILDA Sir?

BERT Are you ... erm ... going out tonight?

HILDA No sir. I shall stay in my room, until ...

BERT Your room? And where is that?

HILDA On the top floor, sir. Second door on the left.

BERT Ah. You don't lock it, do you?

HILDA The door, sir? No, sir.

BERT Ah, jolly good. Thank you.

HILDA Sir ...

Hilda exits.

BERT Crumbs, and to think I didn't believe in Father Christmas.

Rodney has stood up and gone over to the port.

RODNEY Some refreshment, sir?

BERT Oh, thank you.

AGNES I must admit that I am very pleased that you are a vampire, Mr Tomkiss – I do so enjoy meeting people from other walks of life.

BERT Death to be precise.

AGNES So sorry, my mistake.

---

1 shiny, associated with gangsters **2** pacifist

BERT   Oh, it's not too bad – as long as you keep away from the sun and maniacs trying to stick stakes into you. But it's the discomforts that can really get one down. Trying to make your coffin into some sort of home, for instance, without hot and cold running water, toilet facilities or electricity.

Rodney hands Bert some port.

RODNEY   Your port, Mr Tomkiss.

BERT   Oh, thank you. (*Sips*) And it can get really chilly in the winter, even in the day. Sometimes I'd have given my small all for a hot water bottle. And dental hygiene's another thing – these teeth may look impressive, but they get in the way when you try and drink tea and keeping them clean's the devil's own work. They give me gyp[1] whenever I miss and stub them on a bone.

AGNES   I never appreciated that being a vampire was quite so irksome.

RODNEY   I'll say. I always thought it was a glamorous sort of life. In horror films Bela Lugosi[2] just looked at young girls and they did what he wanted – a talent I've often envied . . .

AGNES   Rodney . . .

RODNEY   Sorry dear.

BERT   I've tried that, don't think I haven't, but somehow I've never managed to learn the knack. I've practised staring at milk willing it to change to junket but all I got was a headache. I'm not a vampire by vocation, only by birth. And (*Catch in voice*) . . . if the truth be known, it's a lonely sort of death. People just don't want to know, once you tell them what you are. And even if they did, what can you say? "Come back to my coffin for coffee"? It's hardly the right way to start a friendship.

RODNEY   Steady on, old chap.

BERT   I can't stand it sometimes . . . the loneliness.

AGNES   But, Mr Tomkiss, I always understood that a vampire could make other vampires by . . . well, by biting them in the neck.

---

1 sharp pain   **2** the original stage and screen Dracula, who gave interviews from a coffin and was buried in his costume

BERT   Oh, I know that's the theory, but it doesn't work, not for me . . . not usually, that is. Maybe I'm sterile like that. In fact my only success was with an ex-nun from Stockton-on-Tees, but she didn't last long – went into the bedroom of a choir boy she'd fancied for years just when he'd switched on a sun-ray lamp to give himself a bit of a tan. She was reduced to a little pile of dust in no time flat and the last I knew she'd been swept up and dumped in the garden. Their lobelias[1] came up blood red that year and won first prize in the local horticultural show. Since then I've been totally alone.

AGNES   Oh dear, Rodney. We must help Mr Tomkiss.

RODNEY   Oh, I agree Agnes, absolutely.

BERT   That's very kind of you, but I'm past helping. In fact, the longer I stay here the harder it'll be when I . . . erm . . . well, to put things kindly your butler was distinctly on the scrawny side – hardly seven pints before I was drawing air. And both of you together'll hardly keep me going till morning. Hilda will do very nicely for afters, though – I always like finishing with a virgin, only god knows they're hard enough to find nowadays.

AGNES   Rodney. Mr Tomkiss is looking at my neck.

RODNEY   Have a care, sir. My wife is a married woman.

BERT   You don't happen to be anaemic, do you? I don't want to have to raid a chemist to supplement my diet with jelloids[2].

RODNEY   Our blood, sir, is English to the core.

Bert stands.

BERT   Oh, good. Well now – who wants to be first?

Rodney stands.

RODNEY   Dammit all, sir, I must object. You kill our butler, make eyes at our maid, drink our port, warm yourself by our fire and now you propose to have us for a midnight snack. It's really rather thick.

AGNES   I agree – you should have better manners than to bite the hand that feeds you.

BERT   Neck, to be precise.

---

1 lobelia fulgens – tall with flowers like blood-drops, and toothed leaves   **2** iron tablets

RODNEY   If you carry on in this vein, sir, I shall be forced to ask you to leave the premises.

AGNES   Not that we wish to go to such extreme measures, Mr Tomkiss, but we will if we have to, believe me.

Slight pause. She is struck by a happy thought.

I have an idea. Have you ever thought of entering service?

BERT   Eh?

AGNES   As it so happens we have a vacancy for a butler in our employment.

RODNEY   I say Agnes, what a good idea.

AGNES   I must admit I thought of it the moment I saw Jarvis dead on the floor. You could move your coffin into our attic, Mr Tomkiss, and have our spare paraffin stove for warmth. Working hours could be made flexible in consideration of your nocturnal habits, and if you wished to stretch your wings of an evening the attic has a large window. Nor would you lack for company. There would be myself, my husband, and ... and Hilda.

BERT   Oh, she wouldn't look twice at me.

AGNES   I'm sure she would, dear. My husband and I both know she's highly tolerant of little personal idiosyncrasies. I'm sure that you being a vampire would not upset her in the least.

RODNEY   You little match-maker, Agnes.

AGNES   It would be so nice to have young love blossoming under our roof.

BERT   You're very kind, and the thought appeals, but what would I do for food? I have a somewhat specialised diet, you understand.

AGNES   I have thought of that. We have a friend – a Dr Llewellyn – it so happens that he is in charge of the local blood bank. In exchange for a few gallons daily I'm sure all he would wish to do is take notes on your metabolism, which must be unusual to say the least.

RODNEY   We know for a fact, old man, that he's keen on that sort of thing.

AGNES   It's not everyone that can change into a bat, Mr Tomkiss.

BERT   No no, I appreciate that, but ...

AGNES I do most strongly advise you to take up employment with us; the alternative hardly bears thinking about.

BERT Well ... look, you're both very kind and everything, but I must refuse. Quite apart from the fact mother made me promise never to lower the family name by entering service, I simply can't exist on refrigerated blood – that's as bad for a vampire as baked beans is for normal people. And even if Hilda and I did ... well, get friendly, I'd never forgive myself if I forgot myself one evening and drained her dry.

Opening of door. Hilda enters, with chains.

HILDA Madam – the time ...

AGNES A moment, dear. Is that your final word, Mr Tomkiss?

BERT Yes, I'm afraid it is.

HILDA Madam – sir – the time – the clock is about to strike and I saw Dr Llewellyn's car turn into the drive.

BERT Oh good, another course. I'll leave the YWCA for tomorrow.

He stands. Advances on them.

I'm sorry to have to do this – please don't try to resist ...

Clock starts ting ting tinging midnight.

HILDA Sir – your chains – you must ...

AGNES They will not be necessary, dear – for once we can let the Major have his head.

Transformation noise.

BERT What's happening?

AGNES It is a great pity you picked the night of the full moon to call on us, Mr Tomkiss; my husband is never quite himself on the night of the full moon.

Rodney has metamorphosed into a werewolf. He barks.

And however strong you might be, my husband has even bigger teeth. Rodney!

RODNEY Woof?

AGNES Sic, Rodney, sic[1]!

---

1 Yes, Rodney, really. (Sic) means that an apparent error is intentional.

Rodney growls and leaps at Bert. Fight starts.

I think we had better leave them to it, my dear.

HILDA   Yes, madam ...

They exit. Door closes. Fight noises become muffled.

AGNES   I find the sight of blood excessively unpleasant. I do so hope they don't knock over the trophy cabinet.

The battle, off, has stopped.

Ah – it sounds as if it's over. Just take a peek, dear, and make sure everything's all right.

HILDA   Madam ...

She opens door.

Your husband is sitting on the hearth rug, madam, feeding and wagging his tail.

AGNES   I only hope Mr Tomkiss, poor man, doesn't give him indigestion. Still, it makes a nice change from the cadavers Dr Llewellyn abstracts from the medical school.

Ringing of doorbell.

Ah, there he is. Let him in, Hilda – he'll be ever so sorry to have missed another patient. Still, he can give us a hand clearing Jarvis away.

HILDA   Perhaps your husband, when he's finished with our guest might like to ...

AGNES   Hilda! The very idea! We do not feed the Major on butlers.

HILDA   Sorry madam.

Doorbell again.

AGNES   Do let him in, dear.

HILDA   Madam ...

She opens door.

AGNES   (*to self*) Ah me, what an interesting evening ...
(*Aloud*) Dr Llewellyn, how nice to see you – do come in. You'll never guess what has happened ...

Questions for Discussion and Suggestions for Writing

(Suggestions for writing are marked with an asterisk.)

Maniacs

1　How accurate, exaggerated, or imaginary is this picture of a modern comprehensive school seen through the eyes of the groundsman, boilerman and head?

*　Describe Fred, George and Mr Fish as a pupil might see them.

2　How good do you think Mr Fish is as a headmaster? How far would you agree with George that someone like Fletcher would be better?

*　List the qualities, attitudes and abilities you associate with your ideal headmaster.

3　The original version ended at "Wanting a warm", but the BBC felt this was too macabre. How satisfactory do you find the "only a dream" ending? In what ways does it make the play more convincing, or less effective?

4*　Imagine you are Knackenhead. Write an account of what you did on your last day at school. Explain why you ran away from home. Describe how you spent the time until you reappeared in the "nice little prison" to confront the "boss". Why have you come back?

The Anatomy Class

5　Which student do you sympathise with most, and which least, and for what reasons?

6　In what ways is this picture of higher education similar to your own experience of secondary school?

7　There is a good deal of punning (using words in two senses at once) in this play. Some are explained in the footnotes. Choose a few examples and say how each strikes you. (Amusing, witty, clever, forced, irritating, confusing . . .?)

8*　*Either*
Write out the Lecturer's lines, inserting his own thoughts in

the gaps (about the class, his home life, his position in the college, what he is doing . . .).

Or

Do the same for a teacher giving a lesson to your own class.

En Attendant François

9   Rose thinks the boys have "got the wrong idea". What idea do you think the boys have of the girls? Why do you think they left?

10   What experiences do you have of "blind" dates, first dates, or trying to speak a foreign language? Did you make any humorous or embarrassing mistakes?

11*   Write the conversation the boys have while waiting for the girls, paying the bill, deciding to leave, and writing the note. Assume they are both speaking French and write the English translation (or try it in French).

12*   Write an account, real or imaginary, of a first date or an attempt to speak to a foreigner, bringing out any humour and embarrassment where possible.

Nightmare

13   This play depends for its effect on a quick, unexpected twist at the end. In the broadcast version, the sections marked [. . .] were omitted because of time. How do you think their omission altered the effect?

14   How convincing do you find the ending? We are asked to believe that Drummond burst into the cottage, caused the woman to faint, went to sleep in a bed, and had a nightmare. How did he get in? A car and a knife are missing from the hospital. Who took them?

15   Smith explains "the nightmare just keeps going on". Which parts of the play are nightmare, and which are real? How much of a coincidence is it that a woman and two children, with no man, are staying in the cottage?

16   How would you direct the sound effects and actors to make the play as convincing as possible? Are there any lines you would omit?

17*   Do you have a recurring nightmare? If so, write it out as vividly as possible. If not, describe an imaginary one.

QUESTIONS FOR DISCUSSION AND SUGGESTIONS FOR WRITING

The En Suite Bathroom

18 What reasons has Alan to be so bitter about Joe's financial success? How far do you sympathise with him, and how far do you feel he deserves to be dissatisfied with his life?

19 William Humble suggests that self-employed manual workers earn more than salaried professionals. To what extent is this true? If it is true, why does Joe want his son educated at a public school?

20 Alan describes how he has become the youngest headmaster in the area by "slaving ... at university", "sweating over late Elizabethan poets" and "scrambling up" the teaching scales. His wife is proud of his success, but he feels he has "wasted" eight years of his life.

* Imagine you are Joe. Describe how you learnt your trade, managed in the early years, and now come to enjoy comparative luxury. What are your feelings towards Alan and his wife. What advice would you like to give them?

Tick Tock

21 Because she is unmarried, Louise is expected to care full-time for her disabled mother. She has taken to drinking and has become bitter and resentful. What do you know about the problems of looking after aging relatives, or invalids? How far do you sympathise with Louise, and how far do you think it is her duty to care for her mother instead of putting her in a home? What help is available for people in Louise's position?

22 Louise blames her disappointing life on her parents' "training" of her to accept a "feminine" role. To what extent do you think parents still tend to encourage "healthy aggression" and competitiveness in boys, but "cookery, sewing, *acceptance*" in girls? How far do you think such differences are inborn, and how far are they caused by upbringing?

23 With Mrs Hopkins to do the housework and no need to work for a living, Louise apparently has what many people want: security and someone to care for.

* Write a letter from Cynthia Bowers – whose marriage has failed, whose children are doing badly, and who has money worries – to say how sorry you are about the planned week,

since you desperately needed the break. You envy Louise's lack of financial worries, children, annoying husband, and pressures of work. Say what you would do, in Louise's position, to make life interesting and enjoyable, and to prepare for the freedom she will enjoy when her mother eventually dies.

Taurus

24 What do you know about the Zodiac signs, and how the positions of the constellations and planets are supposed to affect people and events on earth?

25 This is a light-hearted and exaggerated look at what makes people fall in love and marry, but what serious observations do you find here: about compatibility, misunderstanding, decision-making, motives for ambitions and success, how women behave and how men should treat them?

26* Mike has been telling you (a stranger) his story in a pub while drowning his sorrows as usual. Write what you would say, to cheer him up and reconcile him to losing Sandra.

And No Birds Sing

27 Why does Philip lie to the policeman – saying he brought work home when he did not? In what other ways does he seem to incriminate himself, and suggest that "something" did happen in the railway carriage?

28 What indications are there that Ann does not entirely trust or understand her husband?

29 Why do you think the two girls play their "joke"? How malicious do you think they are, towards Philip and towards the police whose time they waste?

30 Read Keats's 'La Belle Dame Sans Merci' in the Appendix and try to explain its relevance to this play.

31* Using your memory and imagination, describe a fellow traveller who struck you as odd, and who amused, frightened or upset you in some way.

Susie Graham's Dance Trophy

32 What reasons can you suggest for Susie's withdrawal into her fantasy world?

33 What does Mrs Graham do to try to help and encourage her daughter? What else might she do – or not do?

34* *Either*

Write an interview, between yourself and an interviewer you admire, about your imaginary success in some field;

Or

Write an article, for a newspaper or magazine you know, about yourself as you hope to be in ten years' time.

Microcosm

35   How does the old man's speaking in a Sheffield accent affect your understanding of what he says, and your impression of his character? Which words show his age? What dialects and foreign or regional accents do you know or recognise? What are their main features? What words do you notice old people using that are no longer current?

* Make a list of regional words with their "standard" equivalents. (In America, "gas" means "petrol", "purse" means "handbag"; in Yorkshire, "'appen" means "perhaps", "owt" means "anything" ....)

* Make a list of old-fashioned words with their modern equivalents. (Cab/taxi, parlour/sitting room, gramophone/record player ...)

36   The old man wonders "what lads are learnin' nowadays, wi' all this automation" and says "There's things can't be read in books, nor fed into computers."

What skills, arts and crafts do you think are dying out because of machines? What new occupations are developing because of increased automation? What need do you see for skilled craftsmen in the future?

How personally satisfying is it to be able to do something well? How important is an absorbing hobby?

37   The old man thinks he has some mysteriously evil power to predict, or even cause, engineering disasters. On the other hand, he says, "That's what engineers make models *for* lad ... ter see 'ow things'll turn out in practice." He is "ahead" of himself, and mischievously thinks of dropping a satellite on Spaghetti Junction.

* While listening to the news of the reactor disaster on the radio, the visitor notices a half-completed model of Spaghetti Junction. Continue the story, either as a play, or in your own words as the visitor.

Mercenary

38 What aspects of life in the army do you find appealing? Which ones do you find distasteful? How does a mercenary differ from a regular soldier? In what ways do you sympathise with Buller?

39 Think of the best three adjectives you can to sum up each character.

40 "Wars provide excitement, comradeship, opportunities for bravery, and employment for weapon-makers and fighters. Military training instils discipline, encourages leadership and decision-making qualities, keeps you fit, and teaches you to use and repair sophisticated equipment. Modern medicine, space rockets and nuclear power owe their development to the threat of war."

 * These are the main points made by the proposer of the motion: "This House believes war is a good thing". Write the speech for the opposition.

The Bognore Regis Vampire

41 Which are the carefully planted hints that the Major is also a supernatural being?

42 This play makes fun of a subject normally treated as horrific. Choose three or four moments when you would expect an audience to laugh, and try to explain why you find them amusing.

43* Using Bert's speeches, especially on page 154, as a model, imagine you are a terrifying monster (out of a book, or from your own imagination) and describe the discomforts and difficulties involved. Write either a letter to a newspaper, or a poem.

The Authors

Ken Blakeson

Ken Blakeson was born in 1944 and lives with his wife and two children in North Yorkshire. After training as a teacher he worked in local radio before becoming BBC Bristol's Education producer in 1970. From 1972 to 1977 he worked as a freelance journalist, broadcaster, writer and teacher, and then started being a playwright as well.

His radio documentaries number thousands, and his work for BBC Radio 4 includes twelve plays, nine schools programmes, a thirteen-part series on *Death and Graves*, many short stories, and writing and introducing the seasonal *Seaside* series. His TV work includes episodes for *Emmerdale Farm* and *Jury*, and three of his musical plays for young children – *Music Hall, The Capture of King Olaf the Silent*, and *The Mask of Mesmera* – have been presented at the Edinburgh Festival.

J. C. W. Brook

J. C. W. Brook started writing in 1973 but now works in computing. His other radio plays include: *Blop, The Nightmare Story of Arnold Pottesbar, Jonas, Blodyn and the Crock of Gold, The Moving of Mr Drimble, The Best of Friends*, and *Giving up*.

David Campton

David Campton was born in 1924 in Leicester, where he still lives. He worked as a clerk with the Leicester Education Authority, a flight mechanic in the RAF during the war, and then for the East Midlands Gas Board. His plays for amateurs started winning prizes in 1954, and in 1956 he became a full-time writer.

Among his many published plays are: *Zodiac* (French) – a spectacular extravaganza for twelve small casts; *Us and Them* (French) – a short and telling comment on war between neighbours for an unlimited cast; *On Stage* and *On Stage Again* (Garnet Miller) which are collections of short plays, sketches and monologues on contemporary themes; *Laughter and Fear* (Blackie Student Drama) containing nine one-act plays; and *The DIY Frankenstein Outfit* (French) – a short comic sketch for nine performers. All are eminently suited to schools and amateurs.

William Humble

William Humble was born in 1948. He studied Drama and Theatre Arts at Birmingham University and, after some teaching, started editing scripts in 1973 for the BBC's *Softly Softly* and *When the Boat Comes In* series. In 1976 he became a freelance writer, and has contributed episodes to many more TV series such as *Flambards*, *All Creatures Great and Small*, and *Juliet Bravo*.

His drama documentaries *On Giant's Shoulders* – about thalidomide boy Terry Wiles – and *Rules of Justice* – about three youths wrongfully accused of murder – received great critical acclaim, and he is now branching out into stage plays and films.

Jill Hyem

Jill Hyem was born in London and used to be an actress. It was during a long run in the West End that she started writing professionally, and since then she has written for radio, TV, stage and screen. She is probably best-known as the co-writer of all three series of *Tenko*, and she has also contributed to *Nanny*, *Angels*, and *Sharing Time*. She has written over forty radio plays, and is a Giles Cooper Award winner. Her published plays are: *Equal Terms* (Evans) for two females, and *Cast-offs* (Evans) for six females – both short.

Maurice Patterson

Maurice Patterson was born in 1932 and lived in a small Kent cottage with no gas, no electricity, no running water and no bathroom. Water came from a well, and the toilet was a bucket in the garden. Despite his parents' poverty he remembers a happy childhood, "playing with trees and haystacks and plants and the world". Although *Susie Graham* seems a sad play he is an optimist, and would like young people to experience more joy. His other radio plays are *Big Deal*, and *Hidden Garden*, and he also writes and directs community drama.

Sam Smith

Sam Smith was born in Liverpool in 1949 and studied Law and Philosophy at Nottingham University, and Philosophy with the Open University. He has not written much yet, but in 1982 his play *Taking the Mickey Sir? Shall I Wrap It For You?* won first prize in the BBC North/West Arts drama competition.

Peter Terson

Peter Terson was born Peter Patterson in Newcastle-upon-Tyne in 1932. He grew up among empty shipyards and dole queues, and left grammar school at fifteen to work in a drawing office. Despite attending the local technical college the mathematics defeated him, so he joined the RAF as a ground wireless mechanic, "washing dishes from Chicksands to Carlisle".

He attented Bristol Training College and taught games for ten years, writing many plays which were rejected. At last, in 1965 *A Night to Make the Angels Weep* was produced at the Victoria Theatre, Stoke on Trent, and in 1966 he became Resident Playwright there. In 1967, two of his plays – *Zigger Zagger* (Penguin Plays) and *The Ballad of Artificial Mash* – won a John Whiting award. Since then he has written many plays, particularly for the National Youth Theatre, specialising in "loose scripts", which leave actors scope for improvisation during rehearsal.

His other stage plays include *The Apprentices* and *Good Lads at Heart*; his TV plays include *The Fishing Party* and *Atlantis*; and his radio plays include *Survey of Imberley* and *Madam Main Course*.

Peter Whalley

Peter Whalley was born in Lancashire in 1946. After teaching for ten years in London and Pontefract, West Yorkshire, he became a full-time writer in 1978 and went back to live in Lancashire. He has written over forty episodes of *Coronation Street*, episodes for *Jury*, and *Angels*, contributions for schools television, and two TV plays – *A Man of Morality*, and *Risking It*. *Maniacs* is one of more than thirty radio plays he has had broadcast, and he has recently published two thriller novels: *Post Mortem*, and *The Mortician's Birthday Party* (both Macmillan).

Ted Willis

Ted Willis was born in Tottenham, Middlesex, on Friday 13 January 1918. His early life – told in his autobiographical *Whatever Happened to Tim Mix* (Cassell) – was spent doing many jobs: baker's roundsman, bakelite moulder, vehicle builder, shop assistant. His first play, *Buster*, was produced in 1944, and he went on to write the stage versions of Richard Gordon's *Doctor in the House* and *Doctor at Sea*, and original West End plays such as *Woman in a Dressing-Gown*, the film of which won eleven awards.

In 1953 he created the famous *Dixon of Dock Green* series for TV, followed by *Sergeant Cork* and many more successes. For his work in the Youth Movement he was created Baron Willis of Chiselhurst in 1963, and as "Lord Ted" is a well-known champion of progressive causes in the House of Lords. He was the first Chairman of the Writers' Guild of Great Britain, which he helped to found. He became a Director of World Wide Film Pictures in 1967, of Capital Radio in 1974, and of Twentieth Century Security in 1981. He also writes novels and radio thrillers.

J. C. Wilsher

J. C. Wilsher was born in London in 1947. He studied at Leicester and Lancaster Universities, and before becoming a writer in 1976 he worked as a research sociologist, a university and adult education tutor, and an armoured van driver for a security firm. He mainly writes scripts for stage, radio and TV, but he also contributes articles to the *New Statesman, New Society* and the *Journal of Social History*. *Microcosm* has been translated into German, and broadcast several times by West German radio stations.

R. D. Wingfield

R. D. Wingfield concentrates mainly on radio drama, and is best-known for his serials and thrillers, although he also writes for TV and light entertainment. He recalls the "constant re-writing and cutting necessary" to get *Nightmare* down to the required length, and prefers to write longer plays "as the BBC pays its writers by the broadcast minute".

Further Reading

ATTENBOROUGH, DAVID   *Zoo Quest Expeditions* – by the popular TV naturalist (Penguin).

BLOCH, ROBERT   *Such Stuff as Screams are Made of* – short stories by the author of *Psycho*, including *The Unspeakable Betrothal* about a young girl's withdrawal from reality (Hale).

BRADLEY, ALFRED editor   *Sound Scene* – ten quarter-hour radio plays selected by the Senior Drama Producer of BBC North (Blackie). *Out of the Air* – five radio plays, with many useful suggestions for producing radio plays in schools (Longman Imprint).

BRIGGS, RAYMOND   *When the Wind Blows* – anti-nuclear black comedy cartoon from the author of *Fungus the Bogeyman* (Penguin).

CAVENDISH, RICHARD   *The Black Arts* – Chapter 5 on Astrology (Pan).

DAHL, ROALD   *A Roald Dahl Selection* – tales from the master of the macabre and unexpected (Longman Imprint).

DOYLE, SIR ARTHUR CONAN   *Sherlock Holmes Meets the Sussex Vampire* – or does he? and other stories (Armada).

GRENFELL, JOYCE   *George, Don't Do That* – hilarious monologues by a primary teacher (Macmillan).

KEATS, JOHN   *Selected Poems and Letters* – edited by Robert Gittings (Heinemann Educational).

MARK, JAN   *Hairs in the Palm of the Hand* – two perceptively humorous school stories (Puffin).

MASTERS, ANTHONY   *The Natural History of the Vampire* – grisly truths behind the legend (Hart Davis).

PEARCE, PHILIPPA   *The Shadow Cage* – ten supernatural tales (Puffin).

POE, EDGAR ALLAN   *Tales of Mystery and Imagination* – from the father of horror (Longman).

REDMOND, PHIL   *Grange Hill Stories* – from the popular TV comprehensive (Armada).

Appendix

La Belle Dame Sans Merci

by John Keats

'O, what can ail thee, knight at arms,
Alone and palely loitering?
The sedge is wither'd from the lake,
And no birds sing.

O, what can ail thee, knight at arms,
So haggard and so woe-begone?
The squirrel's granary is full,
And the harvest's done.

I see a lily on thy brow
With anguish moist and fever-dew,
And on thy cheeks a fading rose
Fast withereth too.'

'I met a lady in the meads,
Full beautiful – a faery's child;
Her hair was long, her foot was light,
And her eyes were wild.

I made a garland for her head,
And bracelets too, and fragrant zone;
She look'd at me as she did love,
And made sweet moan.

I set her on my pacing steed
And nothing else saw all day long;
For sideways would she bend, and sing
A faery's song.

She found me roots of relish sweet,
And honey wild, and manna dew,
And sure in language strange she said,
'I love thee true.'

She took me to her elfin grot,
And there she wept, and sigh'd full sore,
And there I shut her wild, wild eyes
With kisses four.

And there she lulled me asleep,
And there I dreamed – Ah! woe betide,
The latest dream I ever dream'd
On the cold hill side.

I saw pale kings, and princes too,
Pale warriors, death-pale were they all;
They cried – 'La Belle Dame Sans Merci
Hath thee in thrall!'

I saw their starv'd lips in the gloam
With horrid warning gaped wide,
And I awoke, and found me here
On the cold hill side.

And this is why I sojourn here
Alone and palely loitering,
Though the sedge is wither'd from the lake
And no birds sing.'

Longman Imprint Books

General Editor: Michael Marland CBE   ** cassette available*

There is a Happy Land   Keith Waterhouse
Nine African Stories   Doris Lessing
*The Human Element and other stories   Stan Barstow
*The Leaping Lad and other stories   Sid Chaplin
Z Cars   Four television scripts
Conflicting Generations   Five television scripts
*A Sillitoe Selection   *edited by* Michael Marland
*Late Night on Watling Street and other stories   Bill Naughton
Black Boy   Richard Wright
The Millstone   Margaret Drabble
Fair Stood the Wind for France   H. E. Bates
Scene Scripts   Seven television plays
The Experience of Work   *edited by* Michael Marland
Breaking Away   *edited by* Marilyn Davies *and* Michael Marland
The Kraken Wakes   John Wyndham
A Hemingway Selection   *edited by* Dennis Pepper
Friends and Families   *edited by* Eileen *and* Michael Marland
Ten Western Stories   *edited by* C. E. J. Smith
The Good Corn and other stories · H. E. Bates
The Experience of Sport   *edited by* John L. Foster
Loves, Hopes and Fears   *edited by* Michael Marland
A Casual Acquaintance and other stories   Stan Barstow
Cider with Rosie   Laurie Lee
The Pressures of Life   Four television plays
Saturday Night and Sunday Morning   Alan Sillitoe
A John Wain Selection   *edited by* Geoffrey Halson
Goalkeepers are Crazy   Brian Glanville
A James Joyce Selection   *edited by* Richard Adams
Out of the Air   Five radio plays, *edited by* Alfred Bradley
Could It Be?   *edited by* Michael Marland
The Minority Experience   *edited by* Michael Marland *and* Sarah Ray
Scene Scripts Two   Five television plays
Caribbean Stories   *edited by* Michael Marland
An Isherwood Selection   *edited by* Geoffrey Halson
A Thomas Hardy Selection   *edited by* Geoffrey Halson
While They Fought   *edited by* Michael Marland *and* Robin Willcox
The Wave and other stories   Liam O'Flaherty
Irish Short Stories   *edited by* Frances Crowe
The Experience of Love   *edited by* Michael Marland
Twelve War Stories   *edited by* John L. Foster
The Birds and other stories   Daphne du Maurier
A Roald Dahl Selection   *edited by* Roy Blatchford
A D. H. Lawrence Selection   *edited by* Geoffrey Halson
I'm the King of the Castle   Susan Hill
Sliding   Leslie Norris
Scene Scripts Three   Four television plays
Still Waters and other plays   *edited by* Alison Leake
Juliet Bravo   Five television scripts, *edited by* Alison Leake
Television Comedy Scripts   Five television scripts, *edited by* Roy Blatchford
Meetings and Partings   *edited by* Michael Marland
A Laurie Lee Selection   *edited by* Chris Buckton
Strange Meeting   Susan Hill
Looks and Smiles   Barry Hines
Women   *edited by* Maura Healy
Family Circles   *edited by* Alfred Bradley and Alison Leake
P'tang, Yang, Kipperbang and other Jack Rosenthal plays   *edited by* Alison Leake
Humour and Horror   Twelve short plays, *edited by* Caroline Bennitt